CRAFT and PROCESS Studies

Units That Provide Writers with Choice of Genre

Matt Glover

HEINEMANN
Portsmouth, NH

Heinemann

361 Hanover Street

Portsmouth, NH 03801–3912

www.heinemann.com

Offices and agents throughout the world

ISBN: 978-0-325-09973-6

Library of Congress Control Number: 2019943365

Editor: Zoë Ryder White

Production: Hilary Goff, Kimberly Capriola

Cover and interior designs: Vita Lane

Typesetter: Gina Poirier

Manufacturing: Steve Bernier

Printed in the United States of America on acid-free paper

24 23 22 21 20 VP 1 2 3 4 5

Dedication

To my niece Kate,
and all new teachers who create caring schools

CONTENTS

Part One

CHAPTER 1

CHAPTER 2

CHAPTER 3

Part Two: The Units

PROCESS STUDIES

CRAFT STUDIES

Online Resource and Video Contents

**FOR VIDEO CLIPS OF AUTHORS TALKING ABOUT PROCESS,
VISIT WWW.AUTHORTOAUTHOR.ORG.**

How to Access Online Resources

To access the online resources for *Craft and Process Studies*:

1. Go to **http://hein.pub/CraftProcessStudies-login**.

2. Log in with your username and password. If you do not already have an account with Heinemann, you will need to create an account.

3. On the Welcome page, choose **"Click here to register an Online Resource."**

4. Register your product by entering the code: **4GenreChoice** (be sure to read and check the acknowledgment box under the keycode).

5. Once you have registered your product, it will appear alphabetically in your account list of **My Online Resources**.

Note: When returning to Heinemann.com to access your previously registered products, simply log into your Heinemann account and click on **"View my registered Online Resources."**

Acknowledgments

This book is the result of working with literally hundreds of teachers over the last ten years. They have shaped my thinking about the importance of choice of genre. I worry that I will miss thanking someone. Thank you to *all* the educators who have influenced my thinking.

I am incredibly fortunate to have a wonderful friend and editor in Zoë Ryder White. She has helped this book grow from a single chapter in an idea for a different book into a book of its own. Zoë's gentle encouragement nurtures my confidence as a writer.

This book would not have been possible without the writing and thinking of Katie Wood Ray. Everything I know about writing I've learned from Katie, and her detailed feedback on chapters influenced the final form of this book in numerous ways.

Conversations with Isoke Nia and Katherine Bomer provided the foundations for the Independent Genre Study and Using Illustrations and Text to Create Meaning in the Upper Grades chapters. Their thinking helped me see possibilities for units and also helped reinforce important ideas throughout. It was also helpful to be able to talk with friends who spoke the same choice of genre language when I felt like I was living in a land of genres.

Donna Santman also helped me see possibilities for units I hadn't thought of. Her students are lucky to have a teacher who cares so much about choice and engagement. Corinne Arens and some of the teachers she works with helped me think about the unit on planning. Thank you to them for being a laboratory where we could develop new ideas.

Tom Newkirk and Ralph Fletcher were also gracious with their time. Thank you to both of them for being inspirations and championing ideas related to student engagement in their own work.

The numerous video clips throughout the book aim to make visible ideas for making craft and process studies successful. The videos would not have been possible without Kellee Merrit, Emily Foust, and Cherie Colopy. Kellee and the teachers at John Strange Elementary in Washington Township MSD and Emily, Cherie, and the teachers in the Centerville (Ohio) School District made the entire process seamless. Thank you also to the individual teachers who let me use their classrooms and talk with their students.

Thank you to Sherry Day and her Heinemann video crew, Dennis Doyle and Paul Tomasyan, for being so flexible and for understanding what we were trying to capture; to Heinemann Publisher Roderick Spelman; and to Heinemann's production and editorial teams of Sarah Fournier, Catrina Marshall, Patty Adams, Hilary Goff,

Kimberly Capriola, Vita Lane, Maria Czop, Kim Cahill, Steve Bernier, Jennifer Greenstein, Elizabeth Tripp, and Gina Poirier for being endlessly patient and understanding with the details of this book.

Emily Callahan from Quality Hill Academy not only provided additional video but has helped me think about the importance of craft and process studies for many years. Her eager willingness to try out units and push my thinking is invaluable.

There really are too many schools to list, but I'm going to try. I want to thank these schools and teachers for trying out units and turning ideas into strategies that affect children. Their enthusiasm and encouragement provided energy to move forward. Thank you to Sara Ahmed, Beth Dressler, and all the teachers at NIST; Casi Hodge, Lisa Friessen, Chad Sutton, and the teachers in North Kansas City; Corinne Arens, Jenn Phillips, and the teachers and coaches in Blue Springs; Ben Hart, Jill Bellamy, Gill Porteous, and the teachers at American International School of Johannesburg; Ruth Cyrna, Emilie Hard, and the teachers in Issaquah, Seattle; Barbara Rynerson and the teachers at Franklin Roosevelt School; Maya Nelson, Elsa Donahue, and the teachers at Jakarta Intercultural School; Kim Shaw and the teachers in Kansas City, Kansas School District; Alex Campbell, Edel Walshe, and Jen Juteau and the teachers at International School Manila; Sarah Dunkin, Marggi Lowenberg, and the teachers in Beaverton, Oregon; George Dolesch, Tasha Cowdy, and the teachers at International School Basel; Michelle Alzamora, Maureen Carpenter, and the teachers at Anglo-American School Moscow; Krista Babine and the teachers at Kinkaid School, Houston; Lisa Emborsky, Jonathan Johnson, Katie Koenig, and the teachers at American Community School Abu Dhabi; Gail Seay, Lana Al-Aghbar, Katrina Theilmann, and the teachers at the American School of Doha; Geoff Haney and the teachers at Hong Kong International School; Alicia Wilson and the teachers in Platte County; Alice Sikora and the teachers at Zurich International School; the teachers and administrators in Washington Township, Wayne Township, Noblesville, Fishers, and Frankfort, all near Indianapolis; Shanel Catasti and the teachers at Yokohama International School; and Simone Lieschke and the teachers at American International School Guangzhou. Thank you also to Edna Sackson, Jocelyn Blumgart, and the teachers at Mt. Scopus School, and especially to their students Mia Singer and Eden Judah for sharing their wonderful books. I can't wait to read their published writing someday.

Angela Bae and Michelle Baldonado have been particularly enthusiastic and encouraging about the ideas in this book. Thank you for sharing these ideas with the many teachers you encounter.

Kathy Collins, Lisa Burman, Erin Kent, and Kathy Champeu helped reinforce the need for this book. Your enthusiasm provided energy for me to continue writing.

Finally, I want to thank my family—Bridget, Harrison, Meredith, Natalie, and Molly—for helping me remember what is important in education.

PART
ONE

Chapter 1

Increasing Engagement Through Choice of Genre

Early in the school year I often teach a lesson in third to sixth grades on how to find and create independent writing projects. I start the lesson by asking students to share their favorite writing topics and genres, and then I model my thinking about the same topic across different genres. I might show them my own list of favorite topics and then explain how I could write about basketball by writing an informational article about the game, by writing basketball poetry, by writing a fictional story related to basketball, by writing a how-to article on shooting a free throw, or by writing the depressing true story about the time my son beat me in basketball for the first time. The lesson has a fairly predictable rhythm to it, from the audible gasps and excitement when I tell students they are able to write anything they want to the list of predictable topics, with video games always near the top.

Take a look at Video 1.1: Children React to Being Told They Can Choose Their Genre in the Online Resources to see what I mean.

Video 1.1

Children React to Being Told They Can Choose Their Genre

You can see a video of the same lesson with a different group of students in the Online Resources (Video 7.1: Launching Independent Projects [Fourth Grade]).

However, a few years ago when I was teaching this lesson in a typical fourth-grade class, the students' responses were anything but typical. Very quickly we had generated a pretty predictable list of favorite topics: video games at the top, followed by sports, animals, and so on. When I asked them what kinds of genres they liked to write, I was expecting the usual, with fantasy/fiction followed by a few other genres they'd studied. But this class was different.

First, Marcus said, "I like to write parodies."

Me: Really? What do you mean by parodies?

Marcus: I like to take other people's stories and make up my own funny version.

Me: How do you know the word *parody*?

Marcus: My mom taught it to me.

Me: Do you write parodies at school or at home?

Marcus: Oh, only at home.

Next, Sha'naya said, "I like to write sequels." She went on to explain how she takes characters she knows from movies and makes up what happens next (essentially fan fiction).

"Do you do this at school or at home?" I asked.

"Only at home," she said.

Elizabeth offered, "I like to write songs." This one didn't surprise me—this lesson often reveals at least a couple of songwriters.

Next, Jackson said, "I like to write TV shows." He went on to explain that he loves the TV show *Phineas and Ferb*. He records it, and then when he re-watches it, he pauses it and writes down everything the characters say. *He's transcribing entire episodes of* Phineas and Ferb *and then writing his own original episodes.*

→ **Some of the Independent Writing Projects Students Created That Day**

* a personal narrative about playing football

* an essay about why it's not good to have your birthday on Valentine's Day

- a feature article about yellow-bellied sea snakes

- a cookbook for make-believe candy

- a how-to article about how to draw the character Scrat from the Ice Age movies

There were twenty teachers in the room watching this discussion take place. When we debriefed afterwards, the classroom teacher was surprised—she didn't know about her students' writing lives outside school. She said many of the students who spoke up weren't the most confident writers in the classroom, continuing, "The child I was most surprised by was the *Phineas and Ferb* guy. He's the most reluctant writer I've had in twenty-three years of teaching. He hates writing." Kind of an interesting statement about a child who is spending hours a day writing, on his own time! He actually *loves* writing. It's just that his energy for writing is linked to a particular genre. In each of these cases, certain genres affected children's writing energy. In other words, the children's high level of writing engagement was linked directly to a genre that excited them.

In each of these cases, children were on their own to figure out how to capitalize on this energy source. These writing projects lived outside of school, representing what Laura Robb calls "secret writing lives" (Robb 2010). But why should the writing that children invest the most energy in be secret? Children's passions and interests need to be a part of their writing identities at school as well. We tend to be more comfortable making a place for student passion and interest with topic choice, but less so (or not at all) with genre choice. This is a missed opportunity.

If we believe that choice of genre affects engagement, then we must include studies in which students choose their genre. It is crucial that we as teachers align our actions with our beliefs. It's not enough to say that we believe that choice of genre positively affects engagement. If we truly believe this, then we must align our actions by including in each year some units of study that allow for and support choice of genre. And the good news is, this is very possible.

For many children, a *type* of writing is often more enticing than a particular topic. Children who are drawn to fantasy might be attracted to the freedom to create worlds and empower characters with magic. Students who love writing video game guides might be drawn to a genre where they can display a knowledge that has a high level of currency with their peers. Children who write comics might be looking for an avenue to make their friends laugh. In these cases, choosing the topic is often secondary to choosing a genre that feeds a need that isn't being met by other genres.

I've experienced this firsthand as a parent. I have a daughter for whom writing was difficult, and for a long time she was a reluctant writer. She went instantly from low-energy writer to high-energy writer when she had choice of genre. For a while it was songs. When she was twelve she wanted to be Taylor Swift and had

a notebook packed with dreadfully emotional, angst-ridden, teenage songs she had written. Then it was on to movie scripts. She had never had a unit of study on movie scripts, but she somehow figured out what they looked like and started writing a script of a movie she was filming with her friends. Her engagement in writing was *intrinsically linked* with having choice of genre and an authentic purpose.

The Importance of Working Within a Unit of Study

In writing workshop, teaching tends to be organized into units of study that last three to six weeks. We organize our teaching this way so that we can work logically toward meaningful goals, responding directly to what we see students doing each day.

The word *unit* implies that we have goals we are working toward. But the word *study* is just as important. In a unit we are actively engaged in study, or inquiry into how authors create things. While genre study is important, it isn't the only type of study. Units can be organized around any big idea in writing that is worthy of study. A unit could be focused on a *process* authors use, an area of *craft*, or a *genre*.

Unfortunately, increasingly I'm in schools where students never have an opportunity to pursue writing in genres of their choice. A few years ago, I was working in a school district in Ohio that wanted to examine its children's writing experiences from kindergarten through sixth grade. We tracked writing units from K to 6 on a grid so we could see them at a glance. (See Appendix A in the Online Resources for two documents: A1 Unit Data Sample Matrix and A2 Unit Data Blank Matrix.) The first thing we noticed as we studied the grid was that every unit of study, from the first day of kindergarten until the last day of sixth grade, was a genre study. This meant that students would go through seven years of school and over fifty units of study without once having the opportunity to choose their own genre. And in this school this also meant that they would never write fiction, since every story-writing unit was a personal narrative unit.

As I work in schools across the United States and in international schools, I find this increasingly to be the norm. In my experience, this trend coincided with the adoption of new writing standards. Most standards ask students to write different types of texts, but not specific genres. For example, Common Core asks students each year to write in three text types: narrative, informational, and opinion/argument writing. Published programs often responded to these standards by creating units of study that are limited to genres that fit neatly within these text types.

When children have choice of genre, most of the genres they choose on their own *do* align with text types valued by standards. They sometimes choose genres that don't necessarily fit neatly into a text type—but that *do* increase engagement, which is a baseline requirement for a successful and joyful writing life. To be clear, I'm not taking an anti-genre stance. I love genre study, especially studying genres that engage students. Genre study has significant benefits; the most important benefit is that students' understanding about a particular genre—and about writing in general—grows when they study a specific genre in depth over an extended period of time, within the context of a unit of study.

I am also simply pro *study*. The thinking children do when they are studying an idea is very different from the thinking they do when they are simply given information. On the first day of a memoir study, there is a difference between saying, "Here are the two defining characteristics of memoir," and, "Here is a stack of memoirs—let's see what you notice about how they work." In order to think deeply, children need time to deeply study both authors' process and authors' craft. I feel "free-choice" units that are not guided by a particular idea about writing are not very effective. I believe it's important for teachers and students to know what in particular they are studying, whether it is process, craft, or study.

So, that said, this book is not about units of study that turn children loose without support. *This book's biggest goal is to make a compelling case for the belief that choice of genre affects engagement for all writers and to offer support as you act on this belief by including in your year some writing units of study that allow for this choice.*

Many fourth graders I've interviewed, given the choice, would choose some kind of fiction/fantasy writing. But, when I look at schools' units of study in the intermediate grades (and I look at a lot of them), I see that the most underrepresented unit is fantasy. I don't mean that all fourth grades need to include a fantasy-writing unit (although that would be nice); rather, I mean that students must have some opportunities across the year to write in their favorite genres, whatever those might be. It's a hard sell to tell any child at the beginning of the year, "Sorry, I know you really want to write fantasy [or whatever the child's favorite genre is], but we don't study that this year. Hang in there for a whole year and maybe you'll get to write it next year." When my friend Sara's daughter Hanna was in *second grade*, she excitedly told Sara that she would get to write fantasy at the end of *third grade*. Over a year away. And Hanna is a child who loves writing, who writes fantasy and graphic short stories at home. What happens to the children who are less confident, low-energy writers? While this practice is merely unsupportive of Hanna as a writer, it's actually harmful for those who need choice the most.

Choice of genre increases engagement for all writers, but especially low-productivity writers. Teachers often ask me about students who "don't write very much each day" or "don't produce much unless I'm right there with them." The first question I always ask is, "Are they engaged when they have choice of genre, choice of topic, and an authentic purpose?" If a child isn't engaged when these three conditions are in place, then there may be other issues at play (not feeling comfortable with spelling or drawing approximations, being off task throughout the day, etc.). But many students whom we might initially categorize as "low productivity" will dig right in to writing work when they are able to choose what they are making.

Of course, our job as teachers is not only to offer our students opportunities to choose but also to support them as they learn to find their way to both a genre and a topic that engages them. We need to teach them strategies for making *meaningful* choices. I believe that choice is the doorway into meaning. In order to write about ideas that are personally meaningful, students need the opportunity to make significant choices.

Engagement is a prerequisite for a meaningful writing life, which is why the idea of engagement forms the backbone of this chapter on why choice of genre is important. We can, however, make even more of a case for offering units that allow for choice. Here are six additional reasons—all intrinsically linked with engagement—why choice of genre is crucial for all children.

⟶ Units where students choose their genre . . .

- promote authentic purposes and audiences for writing;

- help children better understand the concept of genre;

- accelerate and deepen student learning in the area of study;

- strengthen student writing identity;

- allow students to align genre, topic, audience, and purpose;

- provide teachers with crucial information and understandings about their students as writers.

Reasons for Choice of Genre

1. Choice of genre promotes authentic purposes and audiences for writing.

The opportunity to choose can lead students to discover new, authentic purposes for writing. Interestingly, I've observed that when students are offered the choice, they don't choose *only* their favorite genres. They choose a variety of genres, for a variety of reasons. A few years ago in Kansas City, I was teaching a demonstration lesson in a fourth-grade class that was doing the Finding and Developing Independent Projects unit. I started the minilesson by asking students why they had chosen their genres, assuming we'd hear about their favorite genres and why they chose them. But, as usually happens when I assume too much, the students surprised me. They said:

- "I decided to write a feature article about tornados because I'm scared of tornados and I thought if I learned and wrote about them, I would understand them better and not be so scared."

- "I chose to write a how-to article because my friend said they're really fun to write, so I thought I'd try it out."

- "I chose a fantasy story because I've never written one and I wanted to try something I've never written before."

- "I decided to write a persuasive letter to my parents because I really want a phone."

- "I decided to write poetry because I'm not very good at it and I thought it would be easier to get better at it when we weren't studying it."

That last reason really struck me, so I asked the child to explain. They said, "It's easier to learn something when there isn't the pressure of doing it really well and you are more free to play around with it." That could be a reason all on its own for genre choice: it's easier to learn something when the pressure is low and engagement is high.

In a video earlier in this chapter, we saw a fifth-grade class talk about the variety of genres they liked to write in. In Video 1.3: Fifth Graders Share Reasons for Genre Choice, the same class explains the *reasons* behind their genre choices.

- "I've never written in that genre before. I wanted to do it, but I just didn't think I was smart enough to do it."

- "It's kind of my favorite genre."

- "We have a board in the back of the room with all the different genres, so I looked and chose one."

- "I just watched a really scary movie and wanted to write a scary book."

Video 1.3

Fifth Graders Share Reasons for Genre Choices

Their responses underscore the idea that authors choose genres for a variety of reasons. When genres are always assigned, students won't have experience in choosing genres to match an audience and purpose. If never given the choice, children may not even *know* which genres they prefer. If they've only been exposed to writing a narrow range of genres and they don't find those assigned genres engaging, they may be turned off toward writing in general before they ever find the type of writing that engages them. They may not know if they like to write fiction or poetry unless they have had a chance to give it a try in a low-pressure setting. This is particularly important for low-productivity writers, who especially need genres (and topics) they find engaging. Finding genres they are interested in helps children form writing identities in the early grades and can transform low-energy writers to high-energy writers in the upper grades.

One of our primary goals is for children to be self-directed writers who have the ability to follow their own intentions. We want children to be engaged for reasons beyond the fact that they are required to write. We want them to choose projects because they want to entertain their friends or share what they know about a topic or convince someone to do something. Without the ability and opportunity to find authentic writing projects, it will be more difficult for them to become truly self-directed.

Often in writing conferences I ask children a question that I first heard Shelley Harwayne ask in a workshop years ago: "Where will this writing be two weeks from now?" Basically, she meant, Whom are you going to give this to when you are finished? I recently asked a second grader whom he was going to give his informational soccer book to when he was done. After a long pause he said, "Umm . . . my mom?" I asked if his mom liked soccer and he said, "No, she hates soccer." He wasn't really writing for his mom; she was just the first person who popped in his head.

While we need to teach students how to determine an audience in craft studies, process studies, and genre studies, when children have choice of genre it is easier for them to find an actual person to write for.

In Video 1.4: Roman's Conference: Audience and Purpose, Roman thinks about audience and purpose for his superhero writing. He doesn't initially consider the fact that perhaps someone in his class will want to read it—until his friends help him out by sharing their enthusiasm!

Being thoughtful about audience is an authentic part of the writing process for

Video 1.4

Roman's Conference:
Audience and Purpose

published authors, too. In an NCTE presentation from 2018, Ralph Fletcher talked about the process he used to determine a genre for writing to accompany a series of photographs he took of elephants bathing in a river. After reflecting on all the genres he might choose (photo essay, feature article, literary nonfiction), he decided to write a picture book for children, based in part on his reflections on the bath-time routine of his grandchildren. Writing is about making decisions. It is difficult to learn how to make decisions if one of the most important decisions (choosing your genre) is always made by someone else.

2. Choice of genre helps children better understand the concept of genre.

Simply asking the question "What are you making?" in the context of writing workshop creates the expectation both that children will be making *something*, in a genre of their choice, and that they will know some things about that genre. It requires students to be articulate about genre, especially if we ask them to explain what the genre they've chosen *is* rather than just naming it.

Many teachers include a genre overview study early in their year. One of the goals for the Genre Overview Study described in Chapter 13 is for students to be able to answer the question "What type of book are you writing?" (K–2) or "What type of writing are you working on?" Asking this question automatically communicates the idea that all genres are valued and can be valid choices. Early in this study, many children respond by naming their topic, not their genre. This isn't a surprising response when students have never heard the question—which wouldn't be asked except in the context of a unit that is organized around an idea other than genre. If you were in a realistic fiction unit, you wouldn't ask students to articulate their genre since everyone would be writing realistic fiction.

The question "What are you making?" by nature illuminates children's understanding of genre, which often is not black or white. Katie Wood Ray often talks about the gray area of genre: sometimes a piece of writing has characteristics from several genres, and sometimes you need a lot of words to describe what you're writing, to give the full picture. While it's helpful for students to be able to name their genre, I believe it's more important that they are able to describe what they're making in a way that shows a real understanding of the genre they're writing in. For example, I'm thrilled when a child says, "I'm making a story that didn't happen, but it *could* happen," to describe realistic fiction. That's very different from when a child says, "I'm writing realistic fiction," but they can't clearly state what that is.

Second-grade teacher Emily Callahan often starts the year with the unit We Are Authors and We Make Books. Early in this unit, students are exposed to various genres, and Emily helps children consider what genre they're writing. Each child uses a "Status of the Author" page where they keep track of their titles and genres.

Status of the Author!

Name: _Zoey_

How many books are in your writing folder?	4
How many books have you finished?	3

What kinds of books (genres) have you made?	
Title(s):	Genre:
all abuot me	all abuot
how to make zinez	how to
all about drgon	im comfust becuse it clod be fantycy or all about

Figure 1.1 Zoey's "Status of the Author" Page

Video 1.5
Evie's Intentions

The third entry in Zoey's "Status of the Author" page (Figure 1.1) shows a lot about her understanding of genre. For the genre of her *All About Dragons* book she wrote, "I'm confused because it could be fantasy or all-about." Zoey's grappling with the fact that she's teaching people about a topic that doesn't physically exist in the world, which makes her think it might be fantasy, even though her book is an informational book.

More significant than the correctness of her answer is the very idea that she is thinking about genre in this way. If she was in a fantasy study or an informational study, this deeper thinking wouldn't occur. It's only when she's in a unit where she has choice of genre that she has to consider and describe what she's creating.

Second-grader Evie is also thinking deeply about her genre: she's writing in multiple genres at once. In Video 1.5: Evie's Intentions, you can see Evie explain her plan for her book about her dog, Zoe. Her piece will be built around stories about Zoe, but will include poems about Zoe between each story. When you look at her table of contents (Figure 1.2), you'll see that she's also planning to include some fun facts, so there's an element of informational writing as well. Not only is it unlikely that Evie would have created this multigenre writing in a genre study, but she wouldn't have had the opportunity to pull together what she knows about various genres into a personally meaningful piece of writing. Even if they don't realize it, when students choose their own genre they need to

- consider what genres are available;

- choose a genre that matches their purpose;

- think about the characteristics of the genre (even if they have never formally studied it);

- think ahead or plan their writing in a way that matches their genre;

- try out features and techniques found in the genre.

These are, of course, skills students need in any unit of study. When students engage in this kind of thinking, their understanding of genre strengthens. This deep thinking will also help them when they are studying a particular genre in the context of a genre study. If learning to write in specific genres is such a significant goal that it influences standards and the units of study schools include in a year, then we'd do well to support students' understanding of the concept of genre by allowing them to choose their own genre at various points in the year.

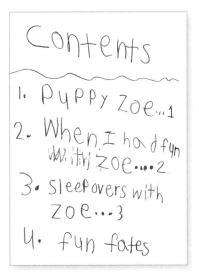

Figure 1.2 Evie's Table of Contents

3. Focusing a unit on a concept other than a genre accelerates and deepens student learning in that area of study.

Engagement alone isn't enough. Students should be engaged in meaningful and valuable experiences. We need to leverage student engagement *to increase student learning.*

The second part of this book is built around specific units based on topics other than genre (craft studies and process studies). The ideas and skills these units are organized around benefit students' writing in any genre. For example, the learning that occurs within an illustration study helps primary students think in greater detail, resulting in more detailed writing across *any* unit of study. The learning that occurs within a unit on crafting with punctuation affects units focused on genres as well. The learning in a unit on reading like a writer will influence students' ability to notice what authors craft and try it in their own writing. All of this is to say, what we teach within units doesn't occur in a vacuum—the goal is for students to internalize new skills that they can use in any writing context.

I'm not much of a camper, but every year during my family's summer vacation in northern Michigan I'm in charge of starting campfires. I *could* carefully construct a small tepee out of kindling around some dried grass, light the grass, and then carefully add larger sticks as the fire grows. However, my regular routine is to throw down some old logs and then douse them with enough lighter fluid that I have to warn everyone to stand back when I throw in a match. My Eagle Scout brother looks on disapprovingly, but the lighter fluid is the perfect accelerant to quickly transform soggy logs to a blaze for making s'mores.

Units focused on ideas other than genre act in the same way as the lighter fluid. They speed up growth in that particular area (without the singed eyebrows). And when we do that earlier in the year, we reap the benefits throughout the rest of the year and beyond. For example, one way to support students' ability to talk about their writing would be to include a peer conferring goal and a couple of minilessons in every unit of study. But another way to get at this goal is to include a unit about having better peer conferences (Ray and Cleveland 2004; Ray 2006), in which students write in the genres of their choice and the unit goals focus around talking about writing. During this unit, students get so much practice that they become substantially better at talking about their writing, in a much shorter period of time. By focusing on one concept (having better peer conferences), students accelerate their learning in that area as they are asked to think about it more deeply during a concentrated period of time. In addition, since students make progress more quickly in the area being studied, they will use that skill at a higher level throughout the year and be even more skilled by the end of the year.

This acceleration occurs in any concept studied in depth. When students are in any craft or process study, focusing conversations on the goals of the study also allows them to see how the crafting techniques and processes they are studying occur in multiple genres. This deepens their understanding of the craft or process and also allows them to use it more effectively during a genre study. We obviously can't focus an entire unit on every craft or process skill, but we can continue to integrate and include a variety of relevant skills in every unit. But including a craft or process study accelerates learning in a particular area in ways that enhance student learning across the year.

4. Units of study in which students can choose their genres strengthen student writing identity.

Recently I was teaching a lesson on finding independent writing projects in a third-grade class in Kansas City. Toward the end of the lesson, I told students they could write anything they wanted. Right away, a boy in the back who hadn't said anything during the lesson quietly asked if he could work on his stories. He went and got a plastic grocery bag from his backpack. Inside was a series of comics—graphic short stories—he had been working on at home. He had them in his backpack because he split time between his mom's home and his dad's home and he wanted to make sure he could always work on them. His writing life was that important to him.

His class wasn't studying graphic short stories, and his teacher hadn't yet learned about the ones he was writing. This opportunity to choose his genre made it possible for his writing identity to be nurtured at school. Fortunately, this boy is in a class with a teacher who values and supports choice of genre and topic. Not only did the teacher honor his writing in the classroom, but the other students now knew that he was working on these books. His writing life became part of his identity as a student, not just as a writer.

Teachers tend to know at least a bit about students' writing lives outside of school, but I wonder, how much are we missing? For every student who will tell anyone who will listen about their stories, how many children are creating pieces of writing that we know nothing about? By including units of study that allow students to choose genres and topics and create anything they want, teachers create an equitable way for all students to enter into the world of writing. *All* students deserve to have their interests and passions heard and valued, and choice of genre should certainly be a possibility not only for certain students but for all students.

Some teachers make sure their students have independent projects, or "backup work" (Ray 2006, 154–56), in their writing folders—writing that they can work on when they have time. Unfortunately, the students who tend to have the most time to work on these meaningful projects are the students who are especially productive writers. The students for whom writing is more difficult or who simply work more slowly will have few, if any, opportunities to work on their independent projects, even though these are also the students who would benefit most from deeper engagement. Units that allow for choice of genre give all students the opportunity to have their writing identities honored and valued.

When students are encouraged to choose what they are making in writing workshop, we are in essence giving them permission to bring their whole selves into the classroom. In a fifth-grade class where students were beginning a unit on finding independent writing projects, I let the children know they could work on any project they wanted. Immediately, Eden and Mia asked if they could work on their story series. They retrieved a shoebox full of books they'd made while the rest of the class knowingly waited to see my reaction. Mia and Eden explained that after reading the book *The Day the Crayons Quit* by Drew Daywalt, they had decided to write their own book, *The Day the Undies Quit*. That led to an ongoing series, including, among many others, *The Day the Undies Regretted Quitting* and *The Day the Undies Were Stolen by the Wicked Wedgie Woman*. They were excited to tell me all about these books as well as their plans for future titles. You can see some of the covers in Figure 1.3.

We want *all* students to have authentic writing lives and to be supported as they write about topics of passion and interest. We don't want the highest-energy writing to be separated from writing workshop. Whether it's songs, TV shows, comics, or a series of stories, we should value what children want to create.

5. Choice of genre allows students to align genre, topic, audience, and purpose.

Decision-making is at the heart of any authentic writing. Authors decide whom they are writing for, why they are writing, what topic they are going to write about, and what genre pulls them all together. It's not enough to choose only topic or choose

Figure 1.3   Covers for Mia and Eden's Undies Series

only audience. Students need at least some opportunities in school to figure out how all four ideas work in concert to create effective pieces of writing.

I started a conference with fifth-grader Jeremy recently with the question "Whom are you writing this for?" thinking I might teach him how to determine an audience. I quickly discovered he was far ahead of me when he responded, "I'm writing a story about the time I adopted my cat. When I'm finished, I'm going to make copies and give it to the people at the cat shelter so they can give it out and maybe other people will adopt a cat." Interestingly, Jeremy's class at that time was working on the unit How to Make Paragraphing Decisions. But, in addition to thinking about paragraphing decisions, Jeremy also

- thought about an authentic reason for writing;

- chose a topic that was personally meaningful to him;

- considered an audience that he cared about;

- decided on a genre that would meet his purpose and resonate with his audience; he considered writing an essay about why people should adopt cats but decided a story would be more personal.

Jeremy could have written about adopting his cat during a memoir study, but his thinking would have been different. Since the genre (memoir) would have been assigned, he wouldn't have had to think about genre possibilities at all. But since he had the opportunity to choose his genre, he could think about all the genre possibilities and decide which genre would be most effective.

Writers make things. Sometimes they write in response to an outside assignment, and other times they initiate a project on their own. In either situation writers benefit from having the opportunity to make choices about every aspect of their writing and to see how those aspects work together.

6. Students' choice of genre provides teachers with crucial information and understandings about their students as writers.

By the end of the first month of school, I want to have a pretty thorough understanding of each of my students as writers. I want to know their favorite topics. I want to know what techniques they use, overuse, and underuse. And I want to know what their favorite genre is. I want to know who the fantasy writers are. Which students write songs. I want to know that Marcus loves writing true stories about his family and that Jacqui loves writing comics. When I know my children deeply, I can better understand how to support their growth.

Second-grade teacher Julie Shisler shared with me her student Audrey's piece on the Great Depression from the first unit of the year (Figure 1.4). The Great

Depression is not your typical second-grade topic! So how did this piece come to be? Audrey and her mom had been reading the American Girl books about Kit, which are set in the Great Depression. I wish I could write like Audrey when I was eight. Think about how much we learn about Audrey from this piece of writing. We have an insight into how she takes complex topics and makes sense of them. We can see what she knows about word choice and structure and endings. We know how she can convey her feelings about a topic. And we know that she enjoys informational writing and teaching others about a topic she cares about.

What's even more significant is what her teacher, Julie, said: if Audrey had been in her classroom the year before, this book wouldn't have existed. In previous years she always started with a unit on personal narrative. This topic wouldn't have surfaced in a personal narrative unit—and it probably wouldn't have come out later in the year in an informational writing unit, either, because even though students would have had some choice of topic, the strategies used for helping students find topics wouldn't have led her to write about *this* topic. Julie is now committed to starting each year with units that allow for genre choice.

I frequently meet children whose disposition toward writing has changed because they had opportunities to choose their own genres. Starting the year with choice of genre can also give us important information about our new class of writers. I was talking about this in a workshop in Indiana recently when teacher Karna Chier said, "At the beginning of the year, I want to understand what my children know about the craft of writing. I want to see what their word choice is like, how they organize their writing, and how they structure sentences. Starting with choice of genre helps me see what my students know." She's right: we learn more about what a student can do in the context of their best writing. A less energizing genre can prompt less engaged and thoughtful writing, and might give us the impression that the child knows less than they do. We want to see what a child can do on their own, right from the start.

Recently I was talking with author Peter Johnston about student engagement. I asked him about the connection between choice and student engagement, whether in reading or writing. His response was "Well, what else is there?" Peter went on to explain that while there are numerous factors that affect engagement, choice is at the top of the list, and that we have to understand the role choice has in fostering true engagement. My hope is that as you think about writing and student engagement, you feel the same way. What else is there?

Figure 1.4 Audrey's Book About the Great Depression

Chapter 2

Choice of Genre Through Craft and Process Studies

Majo is a second grader who loves the Fly Guy series by Tedd Arnold, including *The Old Lady Who Swallowed Fly Guy*. In her book *Fly Guy Is Sick* (Figure 2.1), Majo shows that she learned from Tedd Arnold how to use punctuation to craft the sound of her writing, as well as how to include additional information in the illustrations to help her reader better understand her story.

Yongjin, an English language learner in the same class, also learned how to use his illustrations to convey meaning, but he learned it from Gail Gibbons and the techniques she uses in her book *Sea Turtles*. Yongjin loves Legos, and his class had been studying how Gail Gibbons engages her reader, so Yongjin decided to use a variety of illustration techniques to give his reader additional information in his informational book about Legos (Figure 2.2).

Majo and Yongjin's classmate Sarah loves Bill Martin Jr. After studying several of his books, she decided to model her book's structure after *Polar Bear, Polar Bear, What Do You Hear?* She altered the structure slightly to make it her own in her book *Crab, Crab, What Do You See?* (Figure 2.3), as well as incorporating illustration techniques she learned earlier in the year.

In this Author Study unit, these children and their class studied the craft of Tedd Arnold, Gail Gibbons, and Bill Martin Jr. The unit's main goal was for students to notice specific crafting techniques authors use and try them out in their own writing.

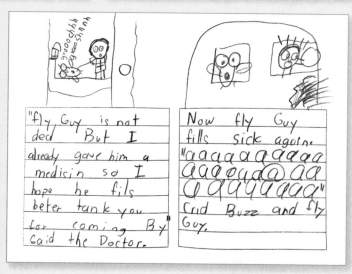

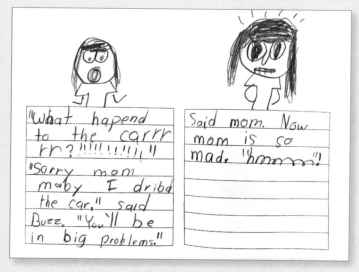

Figure 2.1 Majo's Book: *Fly Guy Is Sick*

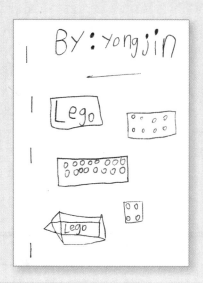

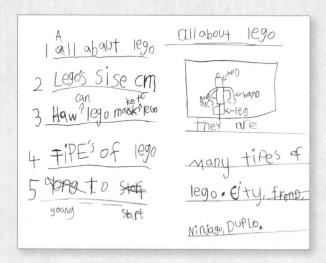

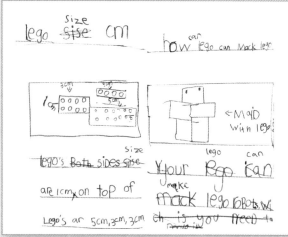

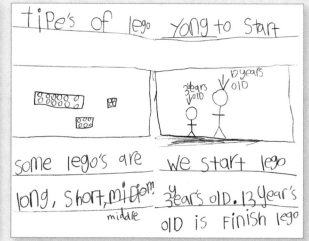

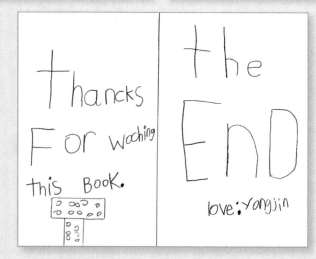

Figure 2.2 Yongjin's Book: *Legos*

Figure 2.3 Pages from Sarah's Book: *Crab, Crab, What Do You See?*

OUCH!!

By: Anisha

It all started with a CRASH! I had fallen off my scooter right onto the sidewalk. I had also fallen onto my left wrist. It hurt so badly it felt like a hammer banging on my wrist. My mom was in Tennessee, my sisters were watching TV, and my dad was talking to the neighbors.

A few minutes later my dad got back and my wrist was starting to get red. My dad asked what happened, and I told him all the details.

And 10 minutes later ya wanna know what I was on my way to the hospital to get and X-ray. It was my first time ever getting an X-ray (hopefully the last time).

About 5-10 minutes later we got to the hospital and we're waiting in the waiting room. If you were wondering we dropped my sisters off to a friends house.

Anyway my name is finally called. By the way I have been to the Urgent Care before, I had gotten a Corneal Abrasion, a scratch in your eye at the time.

So, I get called and we go into the office its huge. It has a bunch of pictures and phrases on the wall. The doctor is a lady not old not young, she has a white coat on a stethoscope around her neck and a smile on her face.

"Hi I'm Dr. Talayna, we'll be going into room 7, just a few rooms down from here", Dr.Talayna said.

When we got to room 7 Dr.Talayna goes through everything about the X-ray and finally we start walking to the X-ray room.

After my X-ray we probably had to wait 20-30 minutes for the results.

Finally Dr. Talayna gets back and she says " I'm afraid that you have broken your wrist". YAY!, I say sarcastically.

After they wrap me up in a cast we get into the car and drive home.

"Finally were home",I say. We get inside the house and after 10 minutes I flop down in my bed and fall asleep.

Figure 2.4   Anisha's Story

It's clear that each of these children has met this goal even though they have chosen to write in different genres.

Though students in this class were studying author craft, a unit might also be organized entirely around a process, such as the unit How Authors Use Conversation to Improve Their Writing. That's the unit students in Christin Forbes' fifth-grade class were working on. Its mini-lessons focused on how to have more productive conversations with a partner. Students kept track of whom they conferred with and what they discussed.

Anderson chose to write an essay to explain to his parents why he wanted a video game system. In a peer conference, his partner, Evan, shared a place where he thought Anderson could add an example and helped him organize the essay into paragraphs.

Anisha was writing a true story about the time she broke her wrist (Figure 2.4). In a peer conference, Anisha asked her friend, Lola, to look at her lead to see if it grabbed her attention. Lola also helped Anisha think about her word choice and not using the same words too frequently.

Kara chose to write a fiction story (Figure 2.5) with different points of view, similar to the book *Wonder* by R. J. Palacio. Kara had said that she wanted help with spelling, so Anisha helped her find some words to fix. Anisha also helped Kara see that a section wasn't needed, so Kara deleted it.

Each of these students chose a different genre but showed evidence of how talking with a peer affected their writing. The genre they chose was secondary to the goal of learning to talk more skillfully about their own writing processes, as learned from studying other authors' processes during this unit. In both of these classrooms, whether students were studying craft or process, they were able to reach the goals and outcomes of the unit while also benefiting from the increased engagement that comes from choosing one's own genre. In addition, students' *wonder*

Kara

I bet you're wondering if I'm going to copy WONDER. No not really I'm not going to make my own story about a boy how always wondered about things and he did many really odd things.Buy I don't want to spoil the story for you that would be boring trust me now,I know you wouldn't want a person spoil a book for you because you would be ~~happening~~. **unhappy** You could be on chapter three and someone told you fred would die and then he's dead in the sixth chapter.If you love happy endings and middels this such the worst book for you to read.If you like happy books too I advise you not to read A series of the unfortunate events either.I am warning you for the last time. DON'T come to me crying and asking me why I made a sad book.Last ~~cans~~. **chance** Ok you haven't put the book down so your ready. Now you can get read for a long drive.

Chapter 1 The big fight

~~Snap~~ your so wrong".
snape

"No I'm not, *LILY* that is my infrince you just think different because you are a different gender.

"That is so rude of you *Why do you hate me I thought we were friends. I bet I WAS WRONG.There is no home for me, nobody understands me,I'm so wrong,why do you hate meeeeeeeeee,bobolesty nobody understands meeeeeeee, I was wronggggggggggg,hah.*"

"Lily not that song again you know where friends you know I care about you."

"How do I know you are just trying not to hurt my feelings ~~snap~~ come on". **Snape**

" Lily you just have to believe me ok"

"Ok".

"Thanks for believing me Lily"

" I never said I believe you I Just want to stop this fight about what happened at school."

"Well we're not going to stop because I want you to trust me". I regeretted what I just had said I should have stoped.So I just went along.Let me give you another summery.

"What ever".

So I was out sid and Jaden the bully was coming at me and I was done being bullied so when he came I punched him in the nutes what's the big deal".

"What's the big deal what's the big deal The deal is that you almost got expelled. "What is wrong with boys erg". "You know what I have to go home so by".

She slammed my door.The house shaked. "Ges what's wrong with girls".

Chapter two what I thought that night

I jumped on my bed and pulled on my covers.I can't sleep so I plane what should happen at school.Thats one thing that's wrong with me I talk aloud and ackt the people and plane what should happen.So here I go.*Me:* Lily I'm sorry what I did yesterday It was so wrong of what I said your the best girl I know *Lily:* I forgive you, and thank you for that nice commplet.*Me:*You know Tomorrow is valentine's day and will you go out with me.*Lily:*oh yes ~~snap~~ I'll go with you I'm sorry what I said to you kissssss.zzzzzzzz.Im am sleep now as you can infer.

Snape

Figure 2.5   Page 1 of Kara's Story

learning increased as they focused on important skills (reading like a writer and talking with others about their writing) for a concentrated period of time.

Elevating Craft and Process Studies

Writing workshop is about studying significant ideas that help children become better writers. Imagine for a moment all the things we could study toward this end. We could study how authors write in a particular *genre* and how the genre works. We could study realistic fiction stories, informational books, commentaries, feature articles, poetry, how-to books or articles, fantasy, literary nonfiction, and on and on. If we can build a stack of pieces of writing in the same genre, then we can study their characteristics and how authors create them.

We could study any aspect of *crafting* texts well. We could study how authors use punctuation, structure, paragraphing, and illustrations to engage their reader in any genre. We could study how one author crafts their texts (author study) or study how authors choose what genre to write in. These studies are focused on the qualities of good writing that cut across genres.

We could also study the *processes* that authors go through as they write. We could study how they find ideas, or plan, or revise. We could study how to be self-directed in writing workshop, find meaningful projects, or talk with others about our writing. These studies are focused on what writers do as they work toward creating finished pieces. Evidence of this work can be less visible, since we can't always see the process that leads to finished pieces. So, in addition to looking at writing, it's important to seek out additional sources of information, such as conversations with students and student reflections on how the process informed their writing.

To support children in becoming strong, confident writers, we need to engage them in *different* types of meaningful studies within and across grade levels. That means we need to elevate craft and process studies to the level of genre studies because all three carry equal importance.

Types of Units

There are three different types of units: craft studies, process studies, and genre studies. In a craft study, the focus is on *what* appears on the page and how authors use techniques to make their writing clear and engaging. We can see evidence of craft on the page. In a process study, we examine *how* authors create pieces of writing. We can't necessarily see the process, but we can see the result of the process in their writing. For example, we can't see the author's revision process in a published piece of writing, though we can see the strong writing that came to be as a result of revising.

Genre studies can be described as the marriage of craft studies and process studies (Ray 2006). When we study a genre, we study both the process authors use to write in a particular genre and the craft they used in the genre (Figure 2.6). Craft and process studies are every bit as valuable as genre studies. In addition to providing the increased engagement of genre choice, craft and process studies involve thinking work that is just as rigorous as that in a genre study. Strong craft and process studies are built around clear unit goals and result in pieces of writing that show what students have learned.

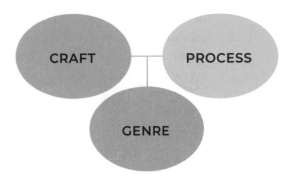

Figure 2.6 Craft, Process, and Genre

How to Include Craft and Process Units

Most of us know that our students would benefit from choosing their own genres, but many teachers work in schools where units are set and there seems to be no room in the school year. I'd argue that even in these situations, you have options. Let's think together about how to include units that allow for choice of genre in a year, in any school community.

Reimagining Existing Units to Allow for Choice of Genre

Often, as you examine the units you already have in place, you'll discover a unit, or units, that *could* allow for choice of genre. The most common example is a unit on launching writing workshop. The goal of a launching unit is independence and self-direction. There's nothing about a launching unit that makes it inherently a genre study, and in fact, students will meet the unit goal of writing independently each day more quickly when they have choice of genre.

It's easy to tweak a launching unit to make it non-genre specific. All you have to do is take out the minilessons that are focused on writing in a particular genre (for example, Finding the Heart of Your Story) and keep or add to the lessons that cut across genres (for example, What to Do When You Think You're Done). You might also have time to add some lessons focused on the goals for the unit or to expand some of the lessons you already have across days.

You might also discover units in your year that are not actually organized around a genre but have been inadvertently turned into a genre study. Units like Launching the *Use* of a Writer's Notebook, Author Study, Revision Study, and Structure, for example, often end up as genre studies unnecessarily. These units and others can be reframed around non-genre-specific goals.

Adding Units to Your Year

Having Four or Five School-Required Units

The easiest-to-adapt scenario is when the year has four or five required units of study. Units of study should generally last 3–6 weeks. It's hard to study anything in depth in less than 3 weeks, especially with an immersion phase and a writing celebration. You *could* study something for just a week, but I wouldn't call that a unit of study. Conversely, if your units tend toward 7–9 weeks, students (and teachers) will be likely to lose energy for the study and will end up studying fewer big concepts in a year.

Even if you did plan for just four units in a year, and each of your units went 6 weeks, that would add up to only 24 weeks of writing instruction. Most schools have 180 days, which equates to 36 instructional weeks (not calendar weeks). Even if you took 10 days out that you don't have writing (field trip days, etc.), that still leaves 34 weeks of instruction. Minus your four required units, that leaves you 10 more instructional weeks—time for at least two units of study that are not focused around genre.

You may be thinking, "If I am to teach everything that is included in the unit my district gave me, it will take 9 weeks." I'd argue here that very few, if any, units, have been designed to take 9 weeks (usually preplanned units include only 20–25 days of writing workshop). When projecting out your own units of study, it's important to plan for fewer than 30 days—and to stick to that plan (Glover and Berry 2012). If you find you need a second or third day on a particular minilesson topic, take out other, less relevant minilessons so that you don't run over. (For more on projecting units, see *Projecting Possibilities for Writers* by Matt Glover and Mary Alice Berry [2012]). See Appendix B in the Online Resources for ideas on keeping units to a manageable length of time.

Having Six to Eight School-Required Units

If you feel your year is already full, with six or more predetermined units, you might consider shaving 3 days off of each—that would give you 18 days that could be used for an additional unit.

You might also swap out an existing unit for a craft study or a process study. If you have eight genre studies in a year, that's a lot of genre study. You probably already have two to three narrative units, two to three informational units, and two to three opinion units. If you decided to include only two units for each text type, that would be more than enough to meet your standards and would also allow you to swap in a craft study and a process study.

Reclaiming Free-Choice Fridays

If your schedule includes "free-choice Fridays" or something similar—an occasional or regularly occurring day when students are able to work on independent writing projects that allow for choice of both topic and genre—you might consider repurposing those days into a craft or process study. I agree that students can and should have independent writing projects and need time to work on them throughout the year. But consider that there are 30–40 Fridays in a year, or about 35 Friday writing workshops. With a little rearranging, that equals time for two 3-week units of study where you'd have the opportunity to organize minilessons around unit goals. Working toward writing goals day by day, rather than over months on multiple Fridays, can bring greater focus.

If your only option, for whatever reason, is to include a "free-choice day" each week, I'd vote for Mondays as opposed to Fridays, so that children start the week with high levels of energy for writing. Starting the week this way also communicates that you value choice in a way that saving it for last, where it has an "if we have time" element to it, does not.

Placing Craft Studies and Process Studies Throughout the Year

As mentioned earlier, units of study tend to last 3–6 weeks, though most genre studies tend to go 4–5 weeks. Craft and process studies tend to be shorter, more in the 3- to 4-week range, since craft and process studies are focused on a few concepts and skills that show up across genres. In craft and process studies, you may or may not decide to teach students how to find ideas, plan, or revise in the same way you do in a genre study. Because craft and process studies are usually shorter, they are easier to fit into certain times of the year or between longer genre studies. It would be harder to include craft and process studies in a packed year if they were 6 weeks long—but luckily, they don't need to be.

The list below shows different ways you might think about balancing craft, process, and genre studies throughout a year. These are not examples or suggestions. Instead, they are just possible outcomes of thinking about the balance of units in your year.

→ **One Possibility for a Year of Studies**

- process study (perhaps launching writing workshop or reading like a writer)

- genre study (perhaps some type of narrative writing, such as realistic fiction)

- genre study (perhaps some type of informational writing, such as literary nonfiction)

- craft study (perhaps a punctuation study, illustration study, or structure study)

- genre study (perhaps some type of opinion-based writing, such as reviews)

- poetry study

- additional study (perhaps a craft study, process study, or genre study)

→ Another Possibility for a Year of Studies

- craft study (perhaps a genre overview study)

- process study (perhaps a revision study or planning study)

- genre study

- genre study

- craft study

- genre study

- poetry study

You can also see one school's units in Appendix A1 in the Online Resources, along with Appendix A2 for a blank matrix to help you think about your units.

There is no ideal ratio between craft and process studies, but I do think it's helpful to intentionally include a balance of both. Rather than focusing simply on the number of units, it's important to consider what the units' goals are and where they are placed in the year. For example, my friend Gill's school had 37 units across K–5: 24 genre studies, 8 craft studies, and 5 process studies. This could appear to be an appropriate balance. But when teachers looked more closely, they noticed that their 5 process studies all occurred as the first or second unit in a grade. While students had plenty of choice of genre in craft studies at other points in the year, the school decided to look at whether they wanted to shift some of the process studies to later in the year.

→ Some Things to Consider as You Choose Units

- How many total units of study are in a year?

- How many of the units are craft studies, process studies, and genre studies?

- Where are units placed in the year, and why?

- Most importantly: Do the number and types of units and their placement in the year align with your beliefs and intentions?

Starting the Year with a Craft or Process Study

Once you've made space in the year, it's time to figure out *when* in the year these units will occur. I believe it's important for students to experience more than one craft study or process study during a year. Requirements for genre studies tend to increase as we move up through the grades, which leads to a situation in which there tend to be more genre studies and fewer craft and process studies in the upper grades. Even so, it's important to offer students some choice of genre *throughout* the grades.

But let's say for a minute that you could only have one unit that allows for choice of genre in your year. If that were the case, I would make a craft or process study my first unit of the year. First, this maximizes engagement and energy for writing right from the start of the year. The first unit sets the tone for the entire year. If students begin the school year writing independently with enjoyment, energy is built for writing across the rest of the year. If you start the year with a genre study, whichever genre you choose, the genre won't engage everyone, making writing more difficult for the unengaged students. As we've already shown, all students don't have the same level of energy for the same type of writing. Starting the year with a craft or process study allows every child to find a genre they have energy for and increases engagement from day one.

Second, choice of genre helps teachers learn more about their writers right from the start. Many teachers choose to start the year with personal narrative study for this reason. While this might help us learn about things students have experienced, I don't think personal narrative helps us understand children *as writers* any more than any other genre does. By the end of the first month of school, I want to know *both* students' favorite genres and their favorite topics. I want to understand each child's engagement level with writing. If I don't, by the end of the first month of school, I may end up digging myself out of a "low-engagement hole." I will know much more about my students in a unit that increases engagement through choice of genre and topic.

In Video 2.1: Scarlett Talks About Her Writing, listen to what we learn about Scarlett, a second grader in Emily Callahan's class, as she talks about her writing early in the year.

- She enjoys writing in different genres.

- She takes risks by trying out a new genre she saw in a book.

Video 2.1

Scarlett Talks About Her Writing

Video 2.2

Kendell Talks About His Voice

Video 2.3

Kendell Reads His Book

- She will initiate independent writing projects.

- She will work collaboratively with a partner to create a book.

- She is confident enough to sing her original song.

- She gets ideas for books from peers in the class.

It's likely that Scarlett's teacher would not have learned any of this if she had started the year with a genre study.

Scarlett is a confident writer, but her classmate Kendell appeared to be less confident in the first week of school, as seen in Video 2.2: Kendell Talks About His Voice. Eventually, Kendell found his way to a meaningful genre and his confidence grew, both in writing workshop and throughout the day. He was inspired by the Who Would Win? series of books by Jerry Pallotta, which led him to write his own Who Would Win? books. Who Would Win? Dab Cat vs. Spiderman (Figure 2.7) included his fictional character Dab Cat, and this book in turn inspired Scarlett to write her book Who Would Win? Tarantula vs. Poisonous Frog. Kendell's cartoon beatbox book, which featured a beatbox battle between Mickey Mouse and SpongeBob, was a big hit with his friends. You can see him read his works in Video 2.3: Kendell Reads His Book.

Making Craft and Process Studies Easier and Effective

When I was young, my friend Chuck and I built a huge tree house in the woods behind our houses. Houses were under construction down the street, so we would go down and pick up nails and discarded pieces of wood. Because we were ten and new to tree house building, we made tons of mistakes. None of the boards between trees

who WOLOD WIN?

DAb CAt VS. SPider Man

by. Kendell

DAbCat can
elchtufie 7 city in
3 secint

spider-Man can
Destroe A biliding
w w w wooooowww
vv

Dab cat can
Run 10000,000
Miles Par Hour

Spider-Man
can Run 10000,000
per Hour too
wow

Blah Blah
Blah Blah

DAb cat can
Rap For 15
Hours Then...

spider-Man
24 Hous
A Day!

DAbcat can FLY
Faster Then FLash
HA HA!

spider-MAN
can FLY
Faster Then
DAb.cat.

DAbcat   size   spider-MAN

Figure 2.7   Kendell's Dab Cat Book

Figure 2.8 Matt's Tree House

were particularly level. Occasionally an entire floor would collapse. It wasn't the prettiest tree house, but we built it all on our own (Figure 2.8).

Later, I built a tree house with my own children. Not wanting the tree house to collapse, I couldn't rely on my building experience as a child to guide me. So, before we started building, I bought a book about building tree houses. It was full of great tips that made building easier. It taught me how to select trees, how to decide on a design, how to minimize damage to trees, and how to ensure the wind wouldn't damage the tree house or trees. The second tree house was both easier to build and more successful because I benefited from the experience of someone else. The book gave me tips to make it easier and traps to watch out for along the way. Teaching a craft or process study for the first time is similar to doing anything new, including building tree houses. New studies will be both easier to implement and more effective with some tips to help the process go smoothly.

Craft and process studies, while they may be less familiar, aren't more difficult than genre studies. The rest of this chapter will share some tips to use and issues to look out for that will make craft and process studies easier for teachers and more effective for students.

Needing Clear Goals for All Units of Study

Any unit of study is more effective when it's built around clear goals. This is as true for craft and process studies as it is for genre studies. Unit goals provide a direction and focus for our teaching and help us keep the unit's purpose firmly in mind as we go.

In *genre studies* (which I'm discussing first simply because they are likely to be more familiar), the unit goals generally focus on authors' craft within the genre and on the processes used to create pieces in that genre.

In *craft studies*, the unit goals focus on evidence in students' writing of understanding the craft being studied, regardless of the genre students choose. For example, in a punctuation study, we expect students to show how they are using punctuation to craft their sentences or phrases in any genre.

In *process studies*, the unit goals will often be revealed in how students talk about their process. The outcomes might be seen in finished products, but often the evidence of process growth is seen in drafts, plans, or students' comments about their process. Process tends to exist farther underground than craft, so we have to dig deeper and look harder. For example, in the How to Have Better Peer Conferences study, the evidence can emerge as teachers observe and teach into peer conferences, students reflect on how their conferences have helped their writing, and students show a place in their writing that was influenced by a conversation with a peer.

Unit	Evidence of Learning
Using Strategies to Find Topics	Students talk about how they find topics. Students find topics rather than telling us they don't know what to write about.
Launching Writing Workshop	Students are self-directed and produce writing independently.
Finding and Developing Independent Writing Projects	Students create independent projects.
Planning	Students show and explain how they planned their writing.
Revision	Students' drafts show evidence of revision, and students talk about the revision moves they made.
How to Have Better Peer Conferences	Teacher makes observations of peer conferences. Students reflect on how their conferences have helped their writing. Students show a place in their writing that was influenced by a peer conference.

We can establish overarching goals for each unit, as well as devise a key question we'll ask students that reinforces the unit goal. Even the unit title and what students share at the end-of-unit celebration can clarify the main goal for the unit. Having a clear goal for the unit helps us stay true to the vision for the particular unit of

Aligning Chosen Genres and Outcomes

When we give children choice of genre, they are able to choose *any genre.* We can't say, "Choose your genre, but only choose certain genres." However, we need to ensure that the genres children choose allow them to demonstrate what they have learned in the unit. For example, the unit goal for How to Have Better Peer Conferences is for students to have better conversations about their writing. Any genre would work for this goal. But, for example, if your fifth-grade students are experiencing the unit How to Make Better Paragraphing Decisions, then they would have to choose genres that have paragraphs.

study and ensure that students will actually have the opportunity to choose their genre. We'll look more deeply at how to choose clear unit goals in Chapter 3.

Ensuring Craft and Process Studies Support Student Choice of Genre

A couple of years ago, I visited a second-grade classroom at the beginning of the year to demonstrate a lesson. The class was in the unit Reading Like a Writer, and when we were getting ready for the lesson before school started, the teacher whose class I was teaching in said, "I'm a bit confused. I gave my students choice of genre, but they're all writing personal narratives." I asked what published texts she had shown the students. She was an experienced teacher and had all her teaching tools handy. All the books she pulled out were personal narratives or sounded like personal narratives.

Then I asked if she had been using samples of her own writing. She had—and they were all personal narratives as well. I asked if she had student samples, and they, too, were all personal narratives. What you expose students to each day, more than anything, influences what they will write. This well-meaning teacher had inadvertently turned the unit into a genre study, simply as a function of the examples she included in her stack. Fortunately, this was an easy problem to solve. We decided to teach a lesson on choosing from a wide range of genres, so I brought a stack of texts from different genres. I started showing students different genres they might write in, and when I pulled out a fiction book, Lucas yelled out, "I love fiction," and they were off to the races.

In addition to making sure you don't inadvertently turn a craft or process study into a genre study, there's another reason to have examples from multiple genres in your stack. In a craft study, the crafting techniques the class is studying show up in multiple genres. It's easier to see how craft cuts across genre when students can see the same craft move in multiple genres. The same holds true for process studies. When you use your own writing in a process study, you can consciously use examples from different genres to model how the process you're teaching is used in each one. For example, in a planning study you might use a different type of graphic organizer to suit each genre you chose, but the main process point is that authors plan their writing in advance, no matter what genre they're writing in.

Of course, the idea that craft and process cut across genre holds true for genre studies also. Recently I was conferring with fifth-grader Gabi, who was in a feature article unit. I asked her, "What have you tried in your feature article that you learned in your poetry study?" (Poetry was her previous unit of study.)

"I don't know," Gabi responded. "It's a different type of writing. I haven't tried anything." I showed Gabi how thinking about word choice in one of my poems influenced word choice in my feature article about tree houses. We talked about skills she had learned in poetry and how she might use those in her article.

The next day, Gabi stopped me in the hall and said, "Mr. Glover, I was thinking about my writing last night. I was thinking that I could talk about these two different types of turtles in my article by going back and forth between them, just like I did in one of my poems." Being able to see how craft and process cut across genres will help Gabi understand that many techniques and skills are not isolated in a genre silo, but rather can be used in multiple types of writing.

Studying Craft and Process

It is much easier for students to study something if they know what it looks like. As teachers we need to be able to show students examples of what they are going to do. There are different ways to show examples.

POSSIBLE EXAMPLES OF WHAT TO STUDY

Unit	Kinds of Examples
Craft study	Stack of published texts that show the craft in various genres
Process study	Video clips, quotations, and possibly published texts showing what authors say about the process
Genre study	Stack of texts from one genre and what authors say about the process of writing in the genre

Stacks of Texts

Teachers of students at any age should be able to answer the question "What are we reading or studying that is like what we're trying to write?" (Ray 2006). There are two key parts to that question. "What are we reading or studying" refers to the stack of published texts we are showing students, and "that is like what we're trying to write" refers to the fact that students are making the same kind of thing they are studying.

In a genre study, the stack of texts is generally composed of four to six pieces of writing from that genre. If students are writing feature articles, then we need to study a stack of feature articles. If students are writing realistic fiction picture books, then we are studying a stack of realistic fiction picture books.

In a craft study, we also need a stack of texts, but the stack is based on examples of the craft we are studying and is composed of more than one genre. For example, in a structure study, we need a stack of books that are crafted with obvious text structures, like Eric Carle's *The Very Hungry Caterpillar* with its days-of-the week structure. We would have multiple structures represented from multiple genres.

Some, but not all, process studies also have a stack of texts from various genres. For example, in the unit Reading Like a Writer, we need a stack of texts that have techniques students can see and try out. And in a unit on finding topics, we need a stack of texts where there is evidence in an author's note about how the author got the idea, or a stack of texts for which we can simply imagine how the author got the idea for the text.

Studying Process with Video Clips, Quotes, Teacher Samples, and Student Samples

There are some process units where the process is not visible in a stack of published texts. For example, in a planning study or a revision study, we can't see the planning or revision moves in the final texts. In these units we can use video clips or quotes of authors talking about their process. We can see what they say about the importance of planning and see their tips for effective planning. Or we can listen to them talk about the importance of revision and the strategies they use as they revise.

To make these clips easier to find, I have created a website with links to clips of authors talking about their process (www.authortoauthor.org). The clips are organized by units of study. My hope is that teachers will help expand the site, contributing links to clips they have used and found helpful. Of course, you could use these clips in a genre study as well, since in genre studies we study the process authors use to create a piece of writing in a genre in addition to studying their craft.

Starting the Unit: Immersion and Setting-the-Stage Lessons

Once you have a stack of texts, students study that stack. I'll use Katie Wood Ray's language here and call this phase of studying the stack of texts an "immersion phase" (Ray 2006).

During the immersion phase, some of the noticing will take place with the whole group as you read a text with the class, point out some things you are noticing, and ask students what they notice. During this phase, you'll generally start an anchor chart of "noticings." The number of immersion days varies depending on the unit of study. The more complex the writing is and the less familiar students are with the unit, the more immersion days you need (maybe 3–4 days). Conversely, if the goals for the unit are easier and students have seen this type of writing before, then you need fewer immersion days (1–2 days).

One exception to using a lesson or immersion phase to start a new unit is the unit Launching Writing Workshop. We want to get students writing right away on day one. If we were to spend two days studying all the routines and procedures of writing workshop, it would be overwhelming. Katie Wood Ray and Lisa B. Cleaveland make this case in their book *A Teacher's Guide to Getting Started with Beginning Writers* (2018).

In *craft studies*, an immersion phase isn't intended to give students a vision for a particular genre. Instead, it's designed to give them a vision for possible ways to include certain craft techniques, regardless of the genre they have chosen. There are benefits to having an immersion phase in a craft study.

- An immersion phase sets the stage for the unit of study. It lets students know what this new unit is about. A couple of days of noticing how illustrations and text work together at the beginning of an illustration study lets students know what the class will be thinking about together over the next several weeks.

- An immersion phase reinforces the importance of inquiry. We want students' habit of mind of noticing what authors do to be more developed in May than it was in September. Craft studies give us yet another important opportunity to strengthen children's ability to notice and try out.

- An immersion phase not only sets the stage for the unit but also acts as an accelerant for students to try things out. For example, if we spend a couple of days noticing interesting punctuation during the first two days of a punctuation study, students will start using more varied punctuation right from the start.

- Along with writing celebrations, an immersion phase creates a clean break from one unit to the next.

In *process studies*, rather than using an immersion phase, I generally set the stage for the unit with a whole-class lesson or two. Since we aren't trying to understand a new genre or do an in-depth inquiry into a stack, we may not need several days of immersion. Like an immersion phase, this kind of "setting-the-stage" lesson helps students know what they will be studying in this unit and gives the unit a clear beginning. Often it's just one writing workshop session where we discuss the big idea for the unit.

For example, in a revision study, on the first day teachers and students might start by sharing experiences with revision: why they like to revise or don't like to revise, what makes revision easier or harder, and how revision is different from editing. The class might watch a few video clips of authors talking about revision or read some quotes of authors talking about how they revise. By the end of this first day of the unit, students have a clear understanding of what they will be studying. Most importantly, they know that they will be showing evidence of the revision moves they will make.

In craft and process studies, helping students understand the goals for the unit will change their thinking and writing right from the start.

Not Needing Examples of Every Genre

Since the goals for the unit of study aren't related to a genre, and since we aren't teaching directly into a particular genre, we don't need to have samples of each genre children have chosen. It's important to include a variety of genres in your stack, but it doesn't matter which genres are included.

Expanding the Range of Genres Children Choose

Recently I taught back-to-back-to-back writing workshops in third-, fourth-, and fifth-grade classes. The third grade was in the unit Launching the *Use* of a Writer's Notebook, the fourth grade was in Finding and Developing Independent Writing Projects, and the fifth grade was in the unit Launching Writing Workshop, all of which allow for choice of genre. In the third grade everyone was writing fiction, except for one girl who was writing an informational article about animals. In the fifth grade every student was writing some sort of fiction story. But in the fourth grade students were writing in nine different genres. The fourth graders were writing

- four realistic fiction stories;
- three biographical sketches (all about soccer players);
- two how-to articles (one about making slime);
- six fantasy stories;

- three personal narratives;

- two feature articles;

- one essay (about why it's bad to have your birthday on a holiday);

- two poetry anthologies;

- three reviews (two video game reviews and one movie review).

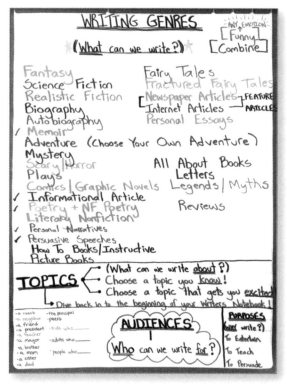

Figure 2.9   Chart of Classroom Library Genre Categories

I see this kind of range frequently but was struck by the difference between the classes. I asked the principal about it, wondering if the difference involved just the particular group of children in this fourth-grade class, and she informed me that each year that teacher's class wrote in a wide range of genres. I asked the teacher why he thought this was the case. He said, "Well, maybe it's because at the beginning of the year we took all the books off our shelves and recategorized them by genre. And we did make a big list of every genre we could think of (similar to the list from Timothy Riley's class. [Figure 2.9]). And I did show them several pieces of my own writing from different genres." Without consciously meaning to, he had opened up genre possibilities, and his class took advantage of the opportunity to choose.

Here are some strategies to make sure your students are actually utilizing choice of genre to choose from a wide range of genres. Remember, it doesn't matter which genres they choose, and we are not trying to influence them in a certain direction. We just want them to actually choose rather than defaulting to the genre that's most familiar.

1. *Have a minilesson early on in the unit that opens up the genre possibilities and shows students how to choose a genre.* You don't have to represent every genre, but it helps to show them that there are a lot of genres they could choose from. You might also ask students what other genres they want to write in. A student doesn't have to have studied a genre in order to be able to try it out. Kindergartners naturally write in a wide range of genres before they have ever studied a genre. And all the students writing songs have likely never had a songwriting unit of study. We want to make sure in this lesson that if students have seen it at all (and even if they haven't), they can try it out.

In every craft or process unit, you will need to decide whether to have a lesson that helps students choose a range of genres. Your students may not need it at all, depending on their previous experiences.

2. *Be mindful about which genre you choose for your own sample writing.* Ideally I would include several samples of my writing from different genres, but I might want to start a new piece in a genre that we haven't studied, to open up that possibility.

3. *Be thoughtful about which student samples from previous years you share.* Again, a range is helpful. I often share pieces with hard-to-define genres.

If we're accustomed to teaching mostly genre studies, the predictable pathway of a genre study can be comforting. You've been there before, you know where the obstacles are, and you know how to get to the end. If you're less familiar with craft studies and process studies, teaching them can at first feel like walking on a path in a forest you've never been in before. You don't know where the challenges are or exactly how the journey will unfold. But without trying a new path, you can't discover something new. Fortunately, as soon as you've made the journey once or twice, this path will feel every bit as familiar and easy to travel as any other.

Chapter 3

Teaching in Craft and Process Studies

While there are many consistencies in how teaching tends to go across writing workshop units in genre, craft, and process studies, you can benefit from becoming aware of teaching processes that particularly support craft studies and process studies in advance of digging in to Part 2, which includes examples of each.

Teaching with a Clear Focus

It's crucial to have a clear vision and purpose for any unit of study, but especially craft and process studies. It's not that the goals of craft and process studies are unclear—it's that we don't tend to be as accustomed to thinking about these goals. Fortunately, there are several strategies for ensuring the teaching goals are clearly defined and understood, including

- identifying the unit rationale;
- carefully naming the unit of study;
- considering key unit questions;
- deciding what will be shared during; the writing celebration.

Identifying the Rationale

Whether you choose a unit of study yourself or your school has made that decision for you, it is important to understand why the unit is important for students. Understanding the rationale will help you

- choose minilessons before the unit starts that work toward standards and unit goals;
- make responsive decisions during the unit about which minilessons to teach based on what you see students doing;
- consider and prioritize teaching points in conferences that work toward unit goals.

Naming the Unit of Study

Naming a unit is actually a significant step in the planning process. You will notice that for all of the units described in Part 2, I have included multiple title possibilities. The more specific the unit's name, the better we (and our students) understand the unit's goals, right from the start. In cases where I've included more than one title, each title describes slightly different unit possibilities. For example, the unit's name can clarify whether a peer conferring unit is focused on conferring just with students or also includes studying a student's role in a conference with a teacher. The name can specify whether a punctuation study is limited to punctuation or encompasses everything writers do with print to affect how their writing sounds.

Key Unit Questions

Another strategy for focusing units is to determine key underlying questions we'll ask in lessons and conferences. A couple of years ago, I was working with a second-grade class that was in an author study of Cynthia Rylant. I went to my first conference of the day and asked the child the unit's key question: *What have you tried in your writing that you learned from Cynthia?* After a long pause the child said, "I have really neat handwriting like Cynthia Rylant." While I'm not sure why he thought that Cynthia's handwriting looks like printed text, at least he had an answer to the question. That was better than if he had said, "Nothing."

But the power of this question comes from its repetition. The first time children hear this question, I don't expect them to answer it thoroughly or particularly well (see handwriting response above!). But after hearing the question repeatedly over time, as they learn more and more about the work of the unit, children start to think more deeply about it in the context of their own writing, and they understand with increasing layers of sophistication that the goal for the unit is to notice an author's techniques and try them out in their own writing. And they begin to do this, which is what we're aiming for.

Unit Outcomes and Writing Celebrations

Publishing means making a piece of writing public. A primary reason to write is to share that writing with an audience, so in addition to sharing day by day with peers, each unit culminates in some type of celebration where students share their writing with students in the class, with another class, with students from another grade, with parents, with office personnel, with the larger community—or with anyone. Keeping in mind the idea of sharing the unit's learning with an audience from the beginning can help us stay focused on the unit's learning goals.

We can reinforce unit goals by planning a celebration that offers opportunities for students to share how they've met those goals. For example:

- In an illustration study celebration, students could share their most interesting illustration decision or show a place where their illustrations and text particularly support each other.

- During a writer's notebook unit, students would share a way they used their notebook to support their writing. They might share their plan for their writing, an entry that helped them find their topic, a place where they tried something out in their notebook, and so on.

- In a peer conferring unit, students could share a place in their writing that was influenced by a conversation with a peer.

- In a revision study, students could explain the thinking behind three of their revisions.

Even though the celebration comes at the end of the unit, it can be helpful to think about what (and how) students will share, right from the start, and to let the students in on it. By clarifying end-of-unit outcomes up front and by linking unit goals to outcomes and celebration, we create and maintain a clear focus for the unit of study.

Who and When: Considering Grade Levels and Time of Year

Grade Range

Many craft studies and process studies are appropriate for any grade from K to 6. But a unit will look very different in different grades, and it's up to us to aim it appropriately. As Katie Wood Ray has said to me, "You don't have to wait for students to be ready for a topic; instead you make the topic ready for the students."

For example, the expectations in a revision study for types and intentionality of revisions are very different for first graders than for fifth graders. First graders might focus more on adding to writing and changing small parts, such as revising for word choice. Fifth graders might focus on the more sophisticated work of deleting sections that don't work toward a central message, or moving parts as they consider effective organization.

Some units, however, are more appropriate for grades K–2 or for 3–6. For example, I generally recommend that students begin using writer's notebooks in grade 3, so I'd personally wait until then for a writer's notebook unit. An illustration study could take place in any grade, but would have a particular impact in kindergarten. A unit on making paragraphing decisions would fit best in grades 3–6, when students are more likely to be writing longer pieces in different genres that need paragraphs. Even within a grade range, a unit may not be as appropriate for a specific grade. It's not that we would rule it out, necessarily, but simply that it might be a better fit in certain grades. For example, you *could* have a punctuation study in kindergarten, but I generally save this for grades 1–6, when students tend to have more writing on the page.

When considering units for specific grades, ask yourself:

- Is this skill important and developmentally appropriate for this grade?

- Can students easily show evidence of the goals for the unit in their writing?

- Are there other units that might be more engaging for this grade?

Time of Year

Many units work well at any point in your calendar. But some might be more effective early on so that students can benefit from the work they do in that unit throughout the year. For example, if a unit on having better peer conferences takes place early in the year, the work done during that unit can increase the quality of students' peer conferences, which supports their writing growth throughout the rest of the year.

In some cases, grade level affects when during the year we place the unit. For example, in the primary grades you might put a revision study later in the year so that students could revisit pieces of writing from earlier in the year. In the upper grades (where students tend to have less of a disposition toward revision), you might put the study early in the year to build students' energy for revision early on.

An additional factor to consider is what genre, craft, and process studies you plan to include in your whole year, and in what order. You might want to space craft and process studies apart so they show up at various points in the year. In kindergarten, I would typically include several craft and process studies at the start of the year before going to a genre study because it's enough for kindergartners to figure out how to get their pictures, text, and oral language to work together in a book, without also trying to understand and write in a genre.

When thinking about where to place a unit in the year, ask yourself:

- Does this unit need to come before another unit? Is there a prerequisite relationship?

- If this unit is placed earlier in the year, will students use and benefit from the skill or technique throughout the year?

- Do students need certain skills before tackling a unit?

- When in the year might students need an especially engaging unit? Should it be the first unit so students can begin the year with high energy? Should it come in the middle of the year, when energy might be flagging?

What and How to Teach

What to Teach in Craft and Process Studies

In any unit of study, only you can decide what your own students need. Standards and curriculum resources can help guide decisions and provide possibilities, but you are the authority on what to teach tomorrow, because you are the person who knows what happened today. It is helpful to have on hand more teaching possibilities than days available in a unit. As Mary Alice Berry and I explore in *Projecting Possibilities for Writers* (Glover and Berry 2012), having a large pool of teaching points supports responsive decision-making about minilessons and makes conferring more effective, especially with students who need specialized support.

In any unit of study (craft, process, or genre), a first place to look for teaching points is your standards and curriculum. Standards are more helpful for determining larger unit goals than they are for planning what to teach in daily minilessons or in a conference. It's helpful to look to additional sources beyond standards. In genre studies, we tend to begin determining teaching points by studying a stack of texts in the genre and creating a list of crafting techniques we notice authors using. We also might study the process authors use to write in that genre. In a craft study as well, we study a stack of texts, but instead of studying texts from *one* genre, we study texts from multiple genres. For example, when preparing for a structure study, we study a stack of texts in various genres that all have predictable, obvious structures, and we notice the structure techniques authors use.

In process studies, teaching points can come from several places:

- studying our own process as writers

- noticing what students do well in their process and what else we would like to see them do

- listening to what published authors say about process
  (visit www.authortoauthor.org)

Whether you study a stack of texts, your own and published authors' processes, or some combination thereof, you'll end up with more teaching possibilities than you can teach in a unit of study. Once you have a pool of teaching points to choose from, you can prioritize which ones you'll teach in minilessons, based on standards, unit goals, and the needs of your class. For a process about how to find teaching points when you are not using a stack of texts, see Appendix C in the Online Resources.

Teaching with Mentors

In genre studies, the mentor texts you gather provide students with examples of the kind of thing they are going to write. But in process and craft studies, the texts you select to support the study serve a different purpose. In craft studies, you'll gather a stack of texts from different genres organized around the craft technique you're studying. For example, in an illustration study, you'll collect a stack of texts across genres in which the text and illustrations clearly support each other. In process studies, you'll also look to mentor authors, but instead of studying texts, you might study what they say about their process.

In any unit, it's important to use teacher writing and student writing (or teachers as mentors and students as mentors). It's never enough to look only at published texts or the work of published authors. Using your own writing is important for several reasons. In order to model reading like a writer (noticing what published authors do and trying it out), you need to do this work yourself. Using your own writing is particularly important in process studies, since an author's process is often invisible in a published piece; for example, we know authors revised, but we can't see the revision work. But we *can* show how *we've* revised in our own writing.

Our own writing also provides students with an *approximation* of published writing. There is no need to make your writing sample as well written as a published author's. Students benefit from seeing our writing as an approximation and as a middle ground between their writing and published writing.

Student writing samples are important as well. They provide students with a picture of what it looks like when someone their age tries out the work of the unit—an even closer approximation to what they are going to do themselves. Using student writing is particularly important in process studies, for the same reason as you'd want to share your writing: process tends to be less visible. Students need to be able to see other students' plans and revisions. They need to see and hear how other student partnerships talk about their writing, or how another student tried something out in their notebook.

Conferring in Craft and Process Studies

Some aspects of conferring are consistent across craft studies, process studies, and genre studies. One of them is to actually teach something during a conference! This sounds obvious, but it can be tricky not to unconsciously fall into reminding, telling, or correcting rather than teaching. A reminder by its very nature means that the child already knows how to do something, so a reminder is just a reminder. Telling a child what to do places the focus on the piece of writing rather than on teaching the child how to be a better writer. And correcting is pointing out what the child doesn't know, rather than showing them *how* to do it. It's not that you should never tell, remind, or correct. But it's important to distinguish teaching from those processes.

The easiest way I can tell if I'm teaching in a conference is by paying attention to whether I use teaching tools (Anderson 2000, 2018). Whenever we confer, we should carry at least these three tools:

- a couple of published texts or the equivalent of published texts (video clips, quotes, etc.)

- samples of our own writing

- samples of student writing

Each of these tools provides different benefits. Published texts show how someone used a technique well (published authors are usually more skilled than we are). Also, published writing is the type of writing students will come in most contact with, so showing published texts strengthens their ability to read like a writer. Not only does teacher writing reveal processes that might be invisible in published work, but also teachers know their own writing best and therefore can talk it through most authentically. Teacher writing also provides that middle ground between published writing and student writing. Student writing, whether it's from previous students or students in your current class, provides different advantages. Some students will be much more likely to try a technique out if they see what it looks like when another student has tried it. And, when I use another student in the class to be the mentor for the child I'm conferring with, this lifts the other child's confidence and status as a writer in the class. You can see me use another child as the mentor in a conference in several conferences, including Video 10.2: Brennan's Conference and Video 10.3: Eli's Conference in the Online Resources.

Here are some tips for building a conferring tool kit—note some differences for craft studies and process studies:

- When saving student writing from year to year in any study, you will want to collect writing at various skill levels, so that all students can see themselves in a piece of writing.

- In any study, your own sample writing should be at a level somewhere between published mentor texts and student writing. Your writing serves as an approximation of published writing and as a more attainable vision for students.

- For craft or process studies, be sure to save student samples from various genres.

- For craft or process studies, best practice is to have multiple samples of your own writing written in different genres. This will help students see how the process or craft skills cut across genres.

- When you are conferring in a craft or process study, carry at least two genres from your stack with you, and keep the rest of your cross-genre stack nearby. You should be able to teach any teaching point with either, or both, pieces of writing since the teaching points aren't genre dependent.

- Remember, you don't need a published, teacher, or student model that matches each student's chosen genre, since you likely won't be teaching into genre.

Deciding on a Teaching Point

In any unit of study, there are many things to consider when deciding what to teach in a conference. What do you know about this student as a writer? What are their personal short- and long-term goals? What did you teach in your last conference with that child? What did you postpone teaching in your last conference (since we should teach only one thing in a conference, there are probably several things you noticed but did not pursue)?

It's also important to consider the goals for the unit you're working in. Minilessons help the whole class work toward unit goals, but conferences meet individual children where they are and help them work toward unit goals in their own way. As we've already established, having clear unit goals helps us focus our teaching, and that holds true in conferences as well. This process looks a bit different in craft and process studies than in genre studies. Let's look at genre studies first.

In a genre study, many goals are related to the specific genre you're studying. Therefore, when you're conferring, one of the first things you're likely to consider is what genre you're studying and how the child is working toward genre-related goals. If the genre goals are being met, or if you see something a child needs more of, *then* you might decide to teach the child a technique or skill that relates to any genre. Basically, when conferring in a genre study, the hierarchy of considerations when determining a teaching point might look like this:

1. Unit goals related to the genre you're studying

2. Unit goals that cut across genres

3. Anything else the child may need

In craft and process studies you'd also think first about unit goals, but in these types of units the unit goals aren't related to a genre. Therefore, in a craft or process study the hierarchy of teaching point considerations might look like this:

1. Unit goals, based on the organizing idea for the craft or process

2. Unit goals that cut across genres

In a craft or process study, teaching into genre won't work toward helping students meet the unit's craft or process goals. It's not that we *can't* teach about the genre. If we can't find anything else to teach, teaching about the genre won't be harmful—but it's likely that you'll discover plenty of teaching points that *will* support the unit's goals before you consider genre-related goals. While this may seem obvious, it can be challenging if you're used to conferring only in genre studies and focusing on the genre right away.

For example, think back to Majo's Fly Guy book described at the beginning of Chapter 2 (Figure 2.1). When I show this piece of writing to groups of teachers and ask them, "What unit of study is this piece from?" 90 percent of the time people guess it's from a unit on writing fiction stories, because that's the genre it's written in. But just looking at the writing doesn't tell us what unit it came from. It could have also come from a punctuation study, an illustration study, a revision study, a study on having better peer conferences, a launching writing workshop study, or an author study (which is the unit the piece is actually from). But most of us are accustomed to seeing genre first, so we assume it's a genre study.

Let's go one step further and think about what you might teach Majo in a conference in different units. The first thing you'd think about is the unit's goals, which depend on the unit. Here are some options:

- Fiction unit: You might first consider narrative fiction teaching points. You might decide to show her how to use dialogue even more effectively.

- Punctuation study: You might first ask her about her most interesting punctuation move and would likely teach into her use of punctuation.

- Author study: You might start by asking what she tried that she learned from Tedd Arnold and then might teach her how to try a new technique Tedd uses.

Your teaching needn't automatically always relate to the unit goals. You might teach Majo something about conventions or using classrooms tools based on her particular needs. But since the unit of study affects our conferring decisions, unit goals are the first element to consider.

Once you've decided on a teaching point, you'll decide on a teaching tool. Since your conferring teaching points will most likely focus on the unit goals, and since unit goals are not focused on a genre, it doesn't matter what genres you have in your conferring kit. As mentioned, you'll want to include a range of genres, but you don't need any particular genre or the genre the child is writing in, so long as you have pieces of writing that reflect what you are working on in this unit. In fact, it sometimes is helpful to intentionally choose to teach with a genre different from the genre the child is writing in, to make clear that the craft or process skill appears in many different contexts. For example, recently I was conferring with a student who was writing an informational book during a punctuation study. I decided to teach him how to use an ellipsis. I had Gail Gibbons' informational book *Frogs* with me, and it has an ellipsis in it right at the beginning. But I decided instead to use a fiction story, which also had an ellipsis in it. I didn't want the student to think that ellipses were found only in informational books, so I intentionally showed it to him in a different genre.

In the videos of conferences appearing in Part 2, you can see both moves—using a sample that is the same genre the child is writing in and using a different genre from the child's. You can also take a look at a list of general conferring tips in Appendix D in the Online Resources.

About Part Two

Paying attention to all these teaching decisions—naming a unit, focusing on unit goals, deciding when to teach certain units, deciding what to teach, conferring, and so on—will make teaching craft and process studies more powerful. In Part 2 you will find overviews of nine process studies and eight craft studies that support writing development, work toward important writing skills, and provide children with opportunities to choose their genre.

Each of the chapters follows a predictable structure and includes the following sections:

- *Unit Title:* Includes multiple versions of unit titles to help you think about your unit focus and goals.

- *Rationale for the Study:* Explains the benefits of the unit and provides a quick overview of the unit.

- *Grade Range:* Indicates which grades might be best for the unit and any considerations about specific grades.

- *Time of Year:* Helps you decide where to place the unit in the year. Many units could go anywhere in the year, but some units have special considerations.

- *Student Learning and the Writing Celebration:* Helps you think specifically about what students will be learning during the unit and how they will show that learning during the writing celebration at the end of the unit.

- *Key Unit Questions:* Helps you think about questions that focus on the heart of the unit.

- *Gathering Published Mentor Texts or Text Equivalents:* Helps you consider what you need in your stacks of texts for the unit.

- *What Might I Teach?:* Provides you with a large pool of teaching points. This section is intended as a starting point to help you envision what you might teach in the unit, not as an exhaustive list of every possible teaching point or recommendations of which teaching points you should select.

- *Conferring:* Helps you think about what to focus on when conferring in the unit and which tools you'll want to have available.

- *For More on This Unit:* Provides you with additional resources to learn more about the unit.

Reminder Boxes

Throughout the chapters in Part 2, you will see reminders about issues that could show up in every unit. Essentially, these reminder boxes represent the most common challenges with craft and process studies. Rather than repeat each reminder in every unit, I have placed them throughout the chapters to occasionally remind you about these ideas. They appear more than once because you might first read only about the units that interest you the most. Here's a quick version of the reminders spread throughout Part 2.

1. Make sure you have more than one genre represented in your stack. However, you don't need to have every genre children have chosen represented in your stack of published mentor texts.

2. Just as you will want to have various genres represented in your stack, ideally you will have student and teacher samples from more than one genre.

3. In any craft or process study, you might need minilessons on choosing genres and choosing topics. If your students are choosing a narrow range of genres, a minilesson or two on choosing genres and picking a genre to go with a specific topic will help ensure students are choosing a genre rather than reverting back to what they have written most recently.

4. You can have teaching points beyond those related to unit goals (planning, revision, conventions, etc.).

5. When conferring, look for teaching points that are related to the unit goals, or that will help students write in *any* genre, before teaching something related to only the specific genre the child has chosen (as a last resort).

6. Having an immersion phase or a setting-the-stage lesson in a craft or process unit accelerates learning and supports students in working toward unit goals right from the start.

7. Using a student in the class as a mentor in a conference with another student lifts the mentor student's status as a writer in the class and boosts their confidence.

8. Remember to phrase key questions as a positive presupposition to communicate to the child that you think they are the type of person who does that type of thing. ("What did you try that you learned from another author?" rather than "Did you try something you learned from another author?")

9. When projecting any unit, it's good to plan for more teaching possibilities than days available. It's helpful to have extra ideas on hand when you decide you need a different lesson from what you had projected, based on what your students need in general. This will also give you a broader range of conference teaching points, which will help you meet diverse individual needs.

10. During the celebration, we want to be careful not to take away from the main goal of sharing and celebrating students' writing. Connecting their writing to the unit goals is important but should be subsidiary to students' sharing.

11. In craft and process studies we're not teaching into any specific genre, so showing a technique in a genre different from what the child is writing in helps the child understand that the same technique can be used in more than one genre.

PART TWO

The Units

The units in Part 2 are meant not to be a comprehensive list of possible craft and process studies, but simply to start you on a path to thinking about unit possibilities that allow for student choice of genre. There are certainly other units you could include in your year that are organized around ideas other than a genre. For example:

- Donna Santman, an incredibly thoughtful teacher, engaged her fifth graders in a unit on specificity. Throughout the unit her students focused on making their writing more precise.

- In her book *Second Grade Writers* (2007), Stephanie Parsons talks about having a unit of study focused on the idea of humor, where students' desire to make their friends laugh would be honored in the classroom.

- I know teachers who have units on beautiful language in which students look at all types of language that makes them pause with admiration.

The possibilities are endless. I hope that the units in Part 2 spark ideas for additional units your students may need.

There are also some units I intentionally didn't include, such as a unit on conventions. I understand the impetus for making this its own unit of study, especially in kindergarten, and if I were going to have a conventions study, I would certainly allow students to choose their genre. But Katie Wood Ray has reminded me that units should foster and nurture growth. Once you know how to write in a conventionally correct way, there's not much more to learn about conventions. Correct spelling is correct spelling. Craft, on the other hand, is limitless and allows for constant decision-making. Rather than including a separate unit on conventions, I would embed goals and minilessons focused on correct conventions in most units of study throughout the year.

My aim for each unit chapter is not to tell you exactly how the unit should go. The teaching points listed in each unit are meant to give you just enough so that you can envision how this unit could work in your own classroom, with your own students. Hopefully I've provided you with enough to spur you to want to read and think more. My goal is that collecting all these units under the larger idea of choice of genre and engagement provides you with enough support to include craft and process studies in your year.

Chapter 4

Launching Writing Workshop: Fostering Self-Direction

or

Independence in the Writing Workshop

or

Routines and Procedures: Launching Writing Workshop

One of the most important elements of writing workshop in general is that it both builds on and supports writers' sense of agency and independence. And how better to support this than with choice of genre? This is as true with kindergartners as it is with older students. When we launch the writing workshop, we're setting the stage for all that's to come for the rest of the year, so it's crucial that we teach students to take charge of their own workshop time.

When Lisa noticed that her kindergartners were frequently interrupting conferences to tell her they were finished, or waiting for her to tell them what to do next, we decided it was time to take these (very predictable) issues on in a minilesson, which you can watch in Video 4.1: Launching the Writing Workshop: Independence (Kindergarten). You'll see that the focus is on creating and using a chart that will support students' independence by offering a process to use when they are stuck or think they're finished. Together we listed four things: one thing to think about when revising, one thing to think about when editing, having a peer conference, and starting a new book. All of these things, we discuss, can be done without telling the teacher! It's important to note that while this lesson takes place in kindergarten, a very similar lesson can be taught in any grade. The specific items on the chart would be different depending on students' needs, but essentially the process is the same, even in fifth or sixth grade: revise/edit what you're working on, have a peer conference, then start something new. Students in grades 3–6 could also put an entry in their notebook or work on an independent writing project when finished.

Rationale for the Study

In this unit you will support children in becoming self-directed, productive writers. We aim for children to be able to work independently for approximately thirty minutes per day. This allows students the writing practice they need and allows teachers to confer with individuals and small groups. Basically, students should be able to run writing workshop by themselves. I often say, "If the teacher faints during writing workshop, students should just step over their body and keep going." And of course, students will write

Video 4.1

Launching the Writing Workshop: Independence

independently more quickly and easily if they are able to choose both a genre and a topic that energizes them.

In *Self-Directed Writers*, Leah Mermelstein defines *self-direction* as a step beyond independence: she says that "being independent is just one small aspect of being self-directed" (2013, 12). The goal is more active than students simply being able to work on their own. We want students to set goals, create plans, solve problems, and find writing projects as they direct their own writing lives.

While independence and self-direction develop throughout the entire year, it helps to start the year with a unit focused on self-direction. In a kindergarten class, the whole first unit typically focuses on routines and procedures because kindergartners have never experienced writing workshop before (a writing workshop structure isn't appropriate in preschool). Devoting an entire unit to supporting students' self-direction is also typical in first and second grades, but in the upper grades students may not need a launching unit if they have already internalized the routines of writing workshop.

→ **You might choose this study if . . .**

- *Your students have never been in a writing workshop before.*

- *Your students have been in a writing workshop before, but you suspect they could use the support of a whole unit to become self-directed.*

- *You're not sure if your students need a whole unit to become self-directed, but you want to play it safe.*

- You want to clearly establish the routines of writing workshop, in any grade.

If students aren't working independently by the end of your first unit, it will be difficult for them to work independently throughout the year. That said, a launching unit isn't mandatory, and if you feel your students really don't need it, you might choose another craft or process study to start the year, such as Reading Like a Writer (Chapter 5), Using Strategies to Find Topics (Chapter 6), or Launching the *Use* of a Writer's Notebook (Chapter 8).

Grade Range

K–6. This unit could be taught in any grade where students need support in being independent and self-directed during writing workshop.

Time of Year

If your students need this unit, you would generally place it as the first unit of the year. If your students need a refresher on what writing workshop looks and sounds like, you may choose to use parts of the unit at other times of the year as needed.

Student Learning and the Writing Celebration

The celebration in this launching unit is crucial to helping students understand that one of the purposes for writing is to share with an audience. In a launching unit celebration, we can connect back to our unit goal by asking students to also share what genre they chose and why, how they found their topic, or something they changed in their writing—anything that relates to the goal of using a process to produce pieces of writing.

Since it's generally the first celebration of the year, it helps to keep it simple. You might just ask students to share their writing in small groups within the class. Depending on the age of the students, they might read their piece, or a part of it, to the class. You might have students share their writing with another class, although you'll have a whole year of celebrations ahead of you, so I tend to suggest something fairly low-key for this first unit.

Key Unit Questions

What have you made since our last conference?

or

What have you created so far today?

or

What challenges have you encountered, and how have you solved them?

These questions all get at the idea of being productive in writing workshop. Some students are often not aware of how much (or little) they are generating during a writing session. Asking what they've created helps students learn to set realistic goals for what they will accomplish in a day and become aware of how their writing process is going. It's important to note that the goal isn't just to write a lot and that volume doesn't equal quality. But, to work on the quality of writing, students must be engaged in the act of writing each day.

Gathering Published Mentor Texts

Much of this teaching unit focuses on writing workshop productivity. In it, you will rely heavily on modeling various routines and procedures. But there will also be teaching points about how to compose texts as well as how to identify and develop a vision for different types of writing. For these teaching points, you will need some published writing to serve as mentor texts. There are several factors to consider as you choose:

* In kindergarten, it's helpful to choose books where the author and illustrator are the same person, just to avoid author/illustrator confusion in the first few days.

- In any grade, you might choose some texts that you know you'll use again later in the year, so that students will know them when they come around again.

- The stack should be composed of multiple genres, including some genres you are not planning to study this year. This helps open up the possibilities for genre choice.

What Might I Teach?

Primary Goals

Students will write productively and independently in writing workshop each day.
   or
Students will use strategies and resources to solve problems they encounter in writing workshop.

Possible Teaching Points

Many of the teaching points in this unit focus on the routines and procedures of writing workshop. However, the goal is to get students writing right from the start. If you spent a week teaching everything students need to know and *then* started having writing workshop, it would be overwhelming and unproductive. Instead, get them up and going and then layer in new routines and strategies each day. In fact, on day one in kindergarten, I say as little as possible—just enough to get them started. Therefore, in this unit I would have an initial short setting-the-stage lesson rather than an immersion phase.

Day One: People Make Books and You Can, Too

In the primary grades, if children have never made books before, the first day is a simple invitation to start putting pictures and words in a pre-stapled book. Read a picture book, referring subtly to various things the author/illustrator did. Then show students some books you've made and some books from last year's class (or other children's examples). Next, show them your stack of pre-stapled books, revealing that there's nothing inside, and let them know that they are going to get to fill them up. And off they go.

If your students have been in writing workshop before, then your first lesson might be on finding topics and genres. It can basically be anything that gets them up and writing right from the start.

Routines, Procedures, and Strategies

- How to start a new book (without telling the teacher your book is finished)

- How to understand that your teacher will decide which books to share each day

- How to add pages to your book

- How to add words to your book

- What to do when your book is finished—using a checklist

- How to not interrupt the teacher when they are conferring with someone else

- How to be productive when you're not interrupting

- How to use classroom resources to solve problems

- What to do with your folder at the end of writing workshop

- How to get started writing quickly

- How to say kind things during share time

- How to talk to your writing partner during minilessons

- How to read your book to your partner before you start a new book

- What to do when your pencil breaks, marker dries out, paper rips, and so on

> In any craft or process study, you might need minilessons on choosing genres and choosing topics. If your students are choosing a narrow range of genres, a minilesson or two on choosing genres and picking a genre to go with a specific topic will help ensure students are choosing a genre rather than reverting back to what they have written most recently.

Composition

While the focus of this unit is independence, we still want students to realize right from the start that writing workshop is all about becoming better writers, so including some minilessons on composition is important.

With younger students, the teaching points will be focused on composing with pictures and words to create meaning in a book. Some minilessons might be

- Staying on topic

- Thinking ahead in your writing

- Reading your book so it sounds like a book

- Using your illustrations to convey more meaning

- Making your illustrations more representative so that you remember what the illustration is and so your book stays more consistent with each reading

- Getting words in your book however you can—scribble writing, random strings of letters, phonetic spelling (the longer students wait to add words, whatever that means to them, the more resistance builds up and the harder it will be for them to start)

With older students, you'll want to establish or strengthen skills they will need all year, such as

- Reading like a writer—noticing and trying out

- How to answer the question, "What have you done in your writing that you learned from someone else?" (published author, teacher as an author, or student author)

- Planning your writing in advance

- Talking with a partner about your writing

- Revising your writing to make it better

- Editing your writing to make it more correct

Possible Lesson Topics: Conventions

You could also include conventions minilessons in this (and every) unit. After conferring with students for a couple of weeks and observing their conventions needs, instead of trying to cover a variety of conventions, I tend to pick one or two things to work on as a class (capitalization, end punctuation, etc.).

Conferring

What to Carry with You

Since you will want students to get in the habit of conferring, you will need tools to confer with right from the start. Carry a couple of texts from your stack of mentor texts, some samples of your own writing, and a few samples of student writing. Student writing will be particularly important so that students start to see what other students' writing looks like. Remember to include a range of student samples, not just samples of particularly skilled writers.

What to Think About While Conferring

Much of the conferring in this unit is focused on productivity and getting to know children. By the unit's end, I want to have a good feel for my students as writers. I want to know students' favorite genres and topics. I want to learn about their confidence as writers and how willing they are to take risks. I want to learn what strategies they use to solve problems.

Your research questions in this unit might be relatively open-ended. In fourth-grader Roman's conference (Video 4.2), I first wonder which genre Roman has chosen, but then ask, "Whom are you going to give this to when you're finished?" Like many students, he hasn't considered whom he's writing for, so I decide to teach him (with the help of some of his classmates) how to decide on an audience for your writing. While this teaching point isn't focused on independence, it is an important idea to address in a first unit so that you establish right from the start that authors write with a reader in mind.

I might also ask some of these questions, depending on children's age and experience with writing workshop:

- What strategies did you use to choose this topic?

- What strategies did you use to choose this genre?

- Whom are you writing this for?

- What was the most challenging thing you have tried in your writing?

- What have you done well in your writing?

- What problems have you encountered?

Stacks of Mentor Texts for Beginning Writers

For very young writers, it's important to choose student samples that show a range of abilities. For student samples of illustrations, you might want

- a book with nonrepresentational illustrations (scribble, "tornado" drawings);

- a book with representational but simple illustrations (for example, a person or object on the page that you can identify, but nothing else);

- a book with multiple objects on the page (for example, a person with background details to show where the person is).

For student samples of words, you might want

- a book with scribble writing;

- a book with random strings of letters;

- a book with beginning phonetic spelling.

Depending on your group of students, you might need a broader or more narrow range. The key is that every child should be able to look at one of the samples and think, "I can do that."

- What can I do to help you become a better writer?

- What are you working on to become a better writer?

- What are your goals as a writer?

- What is your strength in terms of conventions?

- What are your strengths in terms of composition?

Note that the questions are phrased as positive presuppositions, which subtly communicate what we believe about a child. Saying, "What was the most challenging thing you have tried?" is very different from saying, "Have you tried anything challenging?" The first question communicates an assumption that the writer has tried something challenging—it recognizes that writing is not easy. That's especially important for less confident writers who might think that everyone else in the class writes easily. As Peter Johnston (2004) reminds us, the questions we ask communicate what we believe about a person.

Some of the conferences in this unit focus on process and independence, like Meg's (Video 4.3), where I teach Meg how to add pages to her book. Others, like Dom's (Video 4.4), focus on composing. I show Dom how to elaborate in his book by saying more than he has written on the page. Other conferences focus on conventions. In London's conference (Video 4.5), I show her how to say words slowly and write the sounds she hears.

Video 4.2

Roman's Conference

Video 4.3

Meg's Conference on Adding
Pages to a Book

Video 4.4

Dom's Conference on Composing

Video 4.5

London's Conference on Writing
the Sounds You Hear

For More on This Unit

- *About the Authors: Writing Workshop with Our Youngest Writers* by Katie Wood Ray and Lisa B. Cleaveland

- *Engaging Young Writers, Preschool–Grade 1* by Matt Glover

- *Kids First from Day 1: A Teacher's Guide to Today's Classroom* by Christine Hertz and Kristine Mraz

- *A Teacher's Guide to Getting Started with Beginning Writers* by Katie Wood Ray and Lisa B. Cleaveland

- *Self-Directed Writers: The Third Essential Element in the Writing Workshop* by Leah Mermelstein

- *What a Writer Needs*, 2nd ed., by Ralph Fletcher

- *Writing Workshop: The Essential Guide* by Ralph Fletcher and JoAnn Portalupi

Chapter 5

Reading Like a Writer

or

Nurturing the Mindful Habit of Noticing and Trying Out

The ability to notice what other writers are doing and to try those things out in your own writing is one of the most important skills, because once internalized, it sets young writers up to keep learning from writers as they read on their own for the rest of their lives. And when students are able to try out what they're learning in a variety of genres, this solidifies the idea that craft transcends genre and makes what they're learning even more transferrable.

You'll see in Video 5.1: Amari's Conference: Reading Like a Writer (Fourth Grade), that Amari already has the ability to learn from other authors. When I ask the key question "What have you tried in this writing that you've learned from another writer?" she tells me that she learned about word choice from her friend Harper. She even points out a specific place where Harper helped her switch her more typically used *good* for the more specific *delicious*. Amari also talks about learning about repetition (*down, down, down*) from her teacher. Since Amari already has a student mentor and a teacher mentor, I decide to show her a published author mentor: Ralph Fletcher. I read a paragraph from *Marshfield Dreams* and together we find a couple of Ralph's crafting techniques. Amari notices the word *gingersnap* and I point out it's more specific to name the cookie. Even though we're noticing description and word choice, what I'm really showing her is how to notice what a published author has done.

Not only does Amari notice what authors do, but she also applies it to her writing. If you look closely at her writing (Figure 5.1), you'll see that the word *delicious* is no longer there. She changed it later to "rich and creamy." She's using a pair of adjectives, a technique she learned from Ralph's description of his grandmother as "old and tiny." She also changes her second *delicious* to *scrumptious*. This skill of *noticing and trying out* goes far beyond word choice and will assist her in writing in any genre.

Rationale for the Study

One way to learn how to do anything is to study how skilled people do whatever you are trying to learn. My wife, Bridget, and I recently remodeled our bathroom. When we were in the process of picking out a new sink, I couldn't

Video 5.1
Amari's Conference:
Reading Like a Writer

My Pool day

I wake up ealry knowing it is going to be a long I get my sicter's food ready so she does have to wait soon after breakfast I go to the pool with my mom & my sister at the pool I get on a lifejacket and dive into the deep side it was 12 ft down, down, down, I go and I rember I have a life I turn on my back and slowly starting floating back up mely picks me up isky high and throws me up in the air moves out the way and I quikly come down into the the cold water we get out I was running on the edge and full right back into the water I walks up the stairs crawsling up I get up out of the pool and walk up to the snack bar and order three fudge cicles They are rich creamy we hed to the big sand pit get super sandy it felt like I was at the beach we swam until 10:00 pm we ater at MU for dinner It was scrumptius we take a shower and hed to bed thinking that was the best day ever.

Figure 5.1 Amari's Story Revision

help but notice every sink in every restaurant or hotel bathroom. Who knew there was more than one type of sink? Because I now had an image of myself as a bathroom remodeler, I noticed things about bathrooms I liked.

We are never remodeling another bathroom, so my sink-noticing ability will wear off. But in my professional life, I continually need to notice what other authors do. Noticing and trying out writing techniques is absolutely a skill all students (and writers!) need to support them in becoming stronger writers.

Another goal of this work is for students to start experiencing a predictable pattern when they tackle any new type of writing that starts with studying a stack of published mentor texts to understand how the new type of writing works.

Because students will need this skill in every unit, lessons focused on reading like a writer should be embedded in each unit of study throughout the year. However, focusing on this habit of mind for a concentrated period of time will strengthen and accelerate their ability to read like a writer early in the year.

Early on, many students are reading only like readers—for comprehension. Some students notice very obvious techniques, while a few students notice more subtle craft moves. A progression toward thoughtfully reading like a writer might look like this:

1. Students read like readers only, and don't read like writers.

2. Students read like writers and notice techniques authors/illustrators use, but don't try them out.

3. Students notice and try out primarily "easy to notice" techniques.

4. Students notice and try out more sophisticated techniques.

The goal is for students to become more skilled at noticing authors' craft throughout the year and from grade to grade.

- *Your students aren't reading like writers.*

- *Your students are noticing techniques or craft moves but not trying out what they notice.* One of the most common comments I hear from teachers is "My students have become great at noticing craft moves, but the craft isn't showing up in their writing. The focus of a reading like a writer unit is noticing *and* trying out.

- *You want your students to get better at reading like writers.*

Grade Range

K–6. Reading like a writer is an important skill that students need at any age, including in preschool and beyond sixth grade. As students move up through the grades, we expect them to become more sophisticated in what they notice and try out, so this unit could appear in multiple grades in a school, with a different spin as children get older and more experienced.

Time of Year

This unit could come at any point but often appears early in the year. Since students will be reading like writers in most units of study throughout the rest of the year, it makes sense to strengthen this ability early on.

Student Learning and the Writing Celebration

A celebration where students can show their audience what they noticed and tried out is key. One format that works well for this is a gallery walk—students could have their writing out and opened to a particular page and also have the mentor text where they learned the technique right next to it. Students could then share in small groups and talk about several of the techniques they tried and which author they learned the technique from. Older students might also discuss different techniques they considered and why they chose the technique they used.

However you structure it, this should be a celebration of students' ability to notice and try out techniques, in addition to, of course, an opportunity to enjoy their writing.

Key Unit Question

What have you tried in your writing that you have learned from another author (published, teacher, or student)?

This question gets at the heart of this unit. Asking the child what they already "did" as opposed to asking, "Did you try anything out?" communicates that you think they are the type of writer who notices what other authors do and tries those things out in their writing.

Gathering Published Mentor Texts

Even though this is a process unit, you will need texts to teach with so you can model how you notice what authors do and try it out in your own writing.

In K–2, your stack will be composed of picture books since that is what students will be making in the study. In 3–6, it helps to include a range of different types of writing (articles, stories, essays, etc.). You could include picture books in your stack in 3–6, but only if you want students to have the option of making picture books. There are a few things to remember in pulling this stack:

1. Choose writing that will be included in stacks later in the year. For example, a K–2 teacher might include *Long Shot* by Chris Paul because it will show up in their personal narrative unit and *Frogs* by Gail Gibbons because it will show up in the all-about books unit later in the year. In 3–6, you might include your favorite how-to article or fantasy story that students will encounter later in the year during those genre studies. Introducing these titles now will mean students will already be familiar with them during the immersion phase of a subsequent unit. Several pieces of writing may show up in multiple units, which allows students to examine an author's craft and process through multiple lenses.

2. Include some genres that you won't study later in the year so that you give students a vision for as many different genres as possible.

3. Choose texts that include a range of techniques students could actually try out in their writing. When I'm pulling a stack for this unit, as I look through the texts, I imagine what students could notice and try out in their writing. I usually want some texts that have a few fairly obvious techniques as well as a few more subtle techniques. Ideally, I look for texts that include both, like *Roller Coaster* by Marla Frazee, which has easy-to-see techniques like manipulated font and easier-to-miss techniques like a series of three one-word sentences.

Make sure you have more than one genre represented in your stack. However, you don't need to have every genre children have chosen represented in your stack of published mentor texts.

What Might I Teach?

Primary Goals

Students will show evidence in their writing of using techniques they have learned from another author.

This unit's goal is for students to build the habit of mind of noticing what authors do and trying those things out in their own writing. What specifically they are noticing is unimportant—instead, what's important is the intellectual process of noticing and trying out.

Once students are reading like writers, we want them to get better and better at it. Being more intentional in what they try out and explaining their decision-making are signs of becoming more skilled. So a more sophisticated goal might be:

Students will explain their intentional decisions about why they tried out particular techniques they learned from another author.

Possible Teaching Points

Immersion

Since students have already been writing, you might just begin the unit with a series of longer minilessons in which you model reading like a writer and students practice noticing. However, I would recommend beginning with an immersion phase. If you spend a couple of days practicing noticing for the entire writing workshop, both in the whole group and with partners, you will set the stage for the idea that this unit is about noticing what published authors do. On these immersion days, I would also show examples where I have tried out noticed techniques in my writing, and examples of student writing from previous years in which students have tried out techniques.

If you include immersion days, the first day might be spent looking at a text as a whole class as you model noticing techniques. You might then ask students what *they* notice. Students don't write on these immersion days—instead, they focus on noticing and naming what other authors do.

You might start with a text whose techniques are fairly easy to notice. After reading the text as a reader first, model how you notice moves the author made. Begin an anchor chart of noticed techniques. Then ask students what *they* notice, so you are turning the noticing over to them. The amount of teacher modeling will depend on what your particular class needs.

During the immersion phase, I recommend setting students up to notice in partnerships. With a text and sticky notes, partnerships work together to notice and name the techniques in their text. Each partnership might share a noticing with the class. When partnerships share, ask the class if other partnerships noticed the same technique in their book. Since they could be noticing anything, it's likely that other partnerships may not have noticed the same thing, but looking for commonalities lays the foundation for genre studies where we look for common characteristics in a genre.

Modeling the Noticing of Specific Techniques

For a series of minilessons early in the unit, you might model how you noticed a technique and how you tried it in your writing, and/or how other students have tried it in their writing this year or in previous years. This emphasizes the importance of transferring what you notice to trying it out. Some techniques you might notice, depending on your students, could include

- manipulated font size;
- bold print;
- dialogue or speech bubbles;
- beautiful adjectives;
- strong verbs;
- one-word sentences;
- complex sentences;
- similes;
- text and illustration layout;
- illustration techniques (zooming in, background details, etc.);
- exclamation points;
- ellipses;
- beautiful leads or endings.

And on and on. The possibilities are limitless. You and your students might notice anything, and then you'll support them to notice and try subtler, more significant, or more interesting techniques.

Student Noticing

You might include several lessons where you read a text and ask students what they notice. Since you don't know what they may notice, rather than specifically showing your own writing or student writing that uses that technique, you might instead envision aloud for students how you might try it out in your writing. Then students could share how they might try it in their own writing.

Conferring

What to Carry with You

Make sure to include a couple of samples of published writing that you have been using in case you want to show a student a particular technique they could try out. Also include student writing and your own writing so you can model trying out a technique.

What to Think About When Conferring

The first thing to look for in a conference is whether the student is trying out anything they've noticed in the work of other authors (published, teacher, or student). If they haven't, then it makes sense to teach into that, since it's the primary goal for this unit. If the student *is* trying something out, you might teach them how to notice and try out harder techniques, or how to try out a technique and then reflect on whether to keep the revision or not.

In Video 5.1: Amari's Conference, I start with the question, "What have you tried in your writing that you learned from another author?" I want to learn the following:

- Can she identify something she learned from someone else? Amari does, naming word choice.

- Can she name the specific person she learned it from? I want to see if the student is just picking something or if it appears that she can name a specific instance and author. Amari does, naming her friend Harper.

- Does she name composition or conventions? Students will more often go to conventions. Amari names a composition/crafting technique.

- Can she point out a specific spot in her writing? Some students will name something in general, but Amari points out a specific word (*delicious*).

Since Amari is already noticing what student and teacher mentors do and trying those techniques out, I decide to expand her range of mentors by showing her how to notice what published authors do. There are three things to note about this decision:

- I chose a memoir, which happens to be the same genre she's writing in. I could have used any genre, and my teaching isn't dependent on having the same genre as the child. In this case, I just needed a piece that had multiple crafting techniques she could notice, and since I had it handy, I decided to use it. I don't *have* to have the same genre, and I don't *have* to have a different genre.

- Showing her how to notice a published author's crafting techniques supports her as a writer. The type of writing she'll come in most contact with during the year is published text. She'll thus have the opportunity to learn from a greater number of published authors than student or teacher mentors. Each type of mentor provides different benefits, however, so I want her to be able to learn from all three.

- Finally, just having the ability to notice an author's craft doesn't affect a student's writing unless the student tries out some of those techniques in their own writing. On this day I just wanted Amari to notice, but she went farther and applied her "noticings" to her writing.

→ For More on This Unit

- *About the Authors: Writing Workshop with Our Youngest Writers* by Katie Wood Ray and Lisa B. Cleaveland

- *Engaging Young Writers, Preschool–Grade 1* by Matt Glover

- *Independent Writing: One Teacher—Thirty-Two Needs, Topics, and Plans* by M. Colleen Cruz

- *Mentor Authors, Mentor Texts: Short Texts, Craft Notes, and Practical Classroom Use* by Ralph Fletcher

- *What a Writer Needs*, 2nd ed., by Ralph Fletcher

- *Wondrous Words: Writers and Writing in the Elementary Classroom* by Katie Wood Ray

Chapter 6

Using Strategies to Find Topics

or

How Writers Find Topics

or

Beyond Brainstorming: Finding Meaningful Topics

Children often think authors magically come up with writing topics. As you'll see in the beginning of Video 6.1: Minilesson on How Authors Find Topics (Kindergarten), when I ask students how they find ideas, they give very general answers like "I just think of a topic" and "I think about different things." These kinds of answers are also typical for older students, who sometimes think topics are supposed to just pop into their head and often get frustrated when they don't. In this video clip, I teach the strategy "Think about things you really like/love" to help students make the process of finding a topic more visible. I show them how published authors use this strategy, and the students tell me that an author they met, Troy Cummings, also writes about things he loves. I demonstrate using that same strategy, and then the children go off to try it out. Emphasizing the fact that all of us (published authors, students, and myself) use the same strategy nurtures children's identities as authors. After a unit's worth of lessons like this one, students will have a bank of strategies they can use throughout the year, in any genre they choose to write in.

Rationale for the Study

In this unit you'll teach students strategies for finding meaningful topics that will increase their writing engagement. When I encounter a child who isn't writing very much during writing workshop, the first two questions I ask myself are

Video 6.1

Minilesson on How Authors Find Topics

- Does this child have a meaningful topic and genre?

- Does this child have an authentic audience and purpose?

We know choice of genre affects engagement. In addition, children will write with more energy when they are writing *for* someone—when they know their writing will actually go out into the world. Students will also write with more energy when they have a meaningful topic they truly care about. The only way to get to meaningful topics is through choice. Choice is the doorway into meaning-making. If we give everyone the same topic or prompt, *someone* will have less energy for it, no matter what the topic is. In order to find a topic they care about, children must be able to choose it themselves.

However, just because a child has choice of topic doesn't automatically mean they will find a *meaningful* topic. It is our responsibility to teach them strategies for finding topics that matter to them. It's important to note that teaching these kinds of strategies is different from brainstorming topics. When a class brainstorms a list of topics for a unit, generally about 75 percent of the class contributes to the list. Those students already *had* topics in mind. The other 25 percent of the class is looking around at everyone naming topics and is thinking, "How is everyone doing that?" And more often than not, those students end up not liking anything that ends up on the list.

When a child has trouble deciding what to write about, our responsibility is to teach them strategies for finding topics so that from that point forward they will be able to find topics on their own.

→ **You might choose this study if . . .**

- *A large number of your students are having a hard time finding meaningful topics.*

- *You want to help all students find better, more meaningful topics (even the children who already have topics).*

- *You want to increase engagement in writing.*

Grade Range

K–6. Students in any grade K–6 could need support in finding meaningful topics.

Time of Year

This unit often makes sense early in the year so students can use strategies for finding topics throughout the year. However, sometimes students start the year with lots of topic ideas and then energy lags. In that case, teachers might place this unit midyear to boost energy for writing by finding more personally engaging topics.

Student Learning and the Writing Celebration

Since this unit's goal is for students to independently use strategies to find topics, we will want to highlight this process during the celebration. In addition to sharing their writing, students also share the strategy they used to find their topic. This will sound more sophisticated as students get older. A kindergartner might say, "I was thinking about something I like," while a fifth grader might say, "I got the idea by going back through entries in my writer's notebook." During the

> During the celebration, we want to be careful not to take away from the main goal of sharing and celebrating students' writing. Connecting their writing to the unit goals is important but should be subsidiary to students' sharing.

celebration, students might also look at all the strategies students used and figure out which strategies people used most often.

Key Unit Question

What strategy did you use to find your topic?

By asking this question, you are helping students bring to consciousness the strategy they used even if they weren't aware of it as they decided. Being aware of what they did will help them do it more consistently and intentionally in the future.

Gathering Published Mentor Texts

The published texts for this unit could be any piece of writing where the strategy the author used for finding topics is visible. For the younger grades, the author notes at the back of picture books often have information about where the author got the idea. The author note in *Dogs* by Emily Gravett mentions that she has a pet saluki. You might use this book to teach the strategy "Sometimes authors write about something they love."

And in the author's note for *Jabari Jumps*, Gaia Cornwall talks about how she loved to swim when she was little, which reveals the strategy "Sometimes authors get writing ideas when they think about things they like to do." This could, of course, lead to a fiction story or an informational piece of writing, not just a personal narrative. If you get in the habit of reading authors' notes, you will discover lots of strategies authors use.

There are other times when we as teachers can't find direct evidence for why an author chose a topic, but we can make an educated guess. *Frogs* by Gail Gibbons doesn't give us any information about how Gail found the topic. But we could easily say to students, "Gail knows a lot about frogs, so she decided to make a book about something she knows a lot about."

In upper grades we can also use picture books, but in addition we can pull from a variety of different types of writing. We can use strategies like "Authors write about things they know a lot about" whether it is a book, an article, an essay, or some other genre.

We can also use video clips of authors talking about how they find topics (visit www.authortoauthor.org). Another option is to invite a few of last year's students back to our class to talk about how they find topics.

What Might I Teach?

Primary Goal

Students will use strategies throughout the year to find meaningful topics.

Possible Teaching Points

Setting the Stage

In this unit, rather than an immersion phase, you might just have one entire writing workshop focused on the idea of finding topics. You might share your own difficulties in finding topics. You might ask students to talk about times they had a hard time finding topics. Starting this way will help all students, but especially the students who have the hardest time finding topics. On this first day, you could also have students look at a wide range of texts and read authors' notes to find evidence of how the authors found their topics.

Finding Strategies

Much of the teaching in this unit is about strategies for finding topics. One way to think of this is "How could we get the child to talk to themselves (or think about) something that will lead to a writing topic?"

Whenever I have a conversation with a child outside writing workshop, I can't help but think about all the writing ideas that could be sparked by what they're saying. Have you ever heard the expression "If you're a hammer, everything looks like a nail"? Well, I'm that way with topics. A child starts talking about basketball, and I'm thinking, "Have you ever written about basketball?" I have to decide, given the context of the conversation, whether it makes sense to actually say it out loud!

A strategy like "Think about someone who is special to you" doesn't mean the child has to write about someone who is special to them. We aren't using strategies as prompts. But if they *think* about someone who is special to them, that could lead them to all sorts of specific topics. We can model this process ourselves by showing them a piece of our own writing and tracing backwards to where we found the idea and how it led to the topic. For example, in Video 6.1, I model thinking about something I love (my daughter), which reminds me of something I do with my daughter (build with Legos), which leads me to write about the time we built a Lego house and it fell off the table. Older students can do this in a writer's notebook, where they use a strategy to start a bit of stream of consciousness writing to see where it takes them.

Here are some strategies for finding topics you might teach. Some of these strategies are from *About the Authors* by Katie Wood Ray and Lisa Cleaveland (2004).

- Think about something you know about.

- Think about someone special to you.

- Think about someone you know.

- Think about places you've been.

- Think about places you go all the time.

- Think about things you do frequently.

- Think about things you love/like.

- Think about things you're curious about.

- Think about things that have happened to you.

- Think about a time you had a big feeling (really happy, really sad, etc.).

- Think about special memories.

- Think about things you like to do with your friends or family.

- Think about things you know how to do.

- Think about things you care a lot about.

Finding Topics in Your Writer's Notebook (Grades 3–6)

In the upper grades, students might have a writer's notebook where they write multiple short entries each week. These entries can be an excellent source for finding topics. If a child looks back through their notebook and finds multiple skateboarding entries and lists of skateboard tricks, then skateboarding might be a good topic. When children have a favorite topic, or "writing territory," as Carl Anderson (2008) describes topics we tend to write a lot about, they can use that broad topic to find numerous specific topics: skateboarding in general could lead to specifics like an article about how to do a back ollie, a fictional story about a skateboarder, or an essay about why you should be able to skateboard to school.

In their notebook, students could create a web with the broad topics in the middle (skateboarding) and subtopics branching out (skateboard tricks).

A writer's notebook might also include a list of topics or a heart map (Heard 2016) that the child can come back to over and over again to find topics.

General Lessons Related to Topic

You may want to have some lessons that go beyond strategies for finding topics, including

- How to broaden your topic to make it easier to write about

- How to narrow your topic

- When to abandon a topic

- How to tell if you know/remember enough about your topic

- How to keep your audience in mind (for example, by including things you think are obvious that your reader, who doesn't know about your topic, might not know)

- How to keep a list of topics you might write about

- How to use the photos on your writing folder or writer's notebook to generate conversation and find topics

Remember, in a unit like this you could still have some conventions minilessons, or process lessons on planning or revision. All the minilessons don't have to be about finding topics. Most will be, but not all.

Conferring

What to Carry with You

You'll want to bring your own writing, published texts, and student writing. In addition to a range of genres, you will want to include texts that reveal a range of strategies authors used for finding topics. You might have nine pieces of writing that represent nine different strategies for finding a topic.

In the primary grades, you will also want to have an empty pre-stapled book with you that you can use when you are modeling how you are thinking about a topic as you start a new book. In the upper grades, you will need your own writer's notebook to show how you use it to find topics.

What to Think About While Conferring

Keeping your unit goals in mind, you will first want to find out if the child has a topic. If the child does not, then that's certainly what you will teach into. But most of your students will have a topic when you sit down at the conference. Simply having a topic, however, doesn't mean that it will be particularly meaningful or engaging. You might help a student in this situation find a more engaging topic. If the student decides to pursue this new idea, then they can choose to save their current piece of writing for later or abandon it.

When a child does have a meaningful topic, you might ask how they found it, so that they are conscious of the strategy they used to arrive at it. You might also teach into how to narrow or broaden their topic.

If the child seems pretty solid on finding topics, then you could teach them something that would help in any type of writing. This unit might be a good time to ask some questions that usually lead to a teaching point, like

- Whom are you writing this for? Who is your audience?
  (This question often yields a teaching point since many
  children don't have an authentic audience in mind.)

- Why did you choose this genre?

- What are you working on as a writer?

- What are you trying to get better at?

- What are your goals as a writer? What are your goals for this
  piece of writing?

- What have you done well in this piece of writing?

For me, the hardest time to help a child find a topic is during a writing conference. I know that the clock is ticking, which leads to a less natural, interview-like conversation where I feel like I'm just asking questions and trying to pry a topic out of the child. Instead, the best time for me to help a child find a topic is when we're not trying—we're just talking on the way to the lunch room or when the child comes in to start the day. Any time I am talking with a child, topics will pop up naturally, and tucking a "Hey, you could write about this!" into the conversation is invaluable.

→ For More on This Unit

- *About the Authors: Writing Workshop with Our Youngest Writers*
  by Katie Wood Ray and Lisa B. Cleaveland

- *Engaging Young Writers, Preschool–Grade 1* by Matt Glover

- *Heart Maps: Helping Students Create and Craft Authentic Writing*
  by Georgia Heard

- *Strategic Writing Conferences: Smart Conversations That Move
  Young Writers Forward* by Carl Anderson

Chapter 7

Finding and Developing Independent Writing Projects

or

How to Create Pieces of Writing on Your Own Throughout the Year

At the beginning of the year in particular, we want to do all we can to increase energy and engagement in writing in ways that will be self-sustaining throughout the year. Teaching students to design and develop their own independent writing projects, in genres they choose, is one way to do this.

In Video 7.1: Launching Independent Projects (Fourth Grade), you'll see one way to launch this unit in a fourth-grade classroom early in the year. Starting with a list of students' favorite topics, we continue by listing their favorite genres. I help expand the possibilities by showing some potentially less familiar genres. Using one student's favorite topic—history, specifically the year 1865—we consider how he could write poetry or a graphic short story about the end of slavery, a historical fiction story set in 1865, a biographical sketch of Abraham Lincoln, or an essay about why 1865 is the most important year. We end by having a couple of students share what they are going to make. This lesson could have been stretched out over several days, with one day on trying all sorts of strategies for finding topics and another on doing a deeper investigation into possible genres. The third day could have focused on choosing a topic and genre, and then thinking about audience and purpose. What's important to notice is the palpable excitement for creating their own projects that comes when students are supported in this kind of work.

Rationale for the Study

Video 7.1

Launching Independent Projects

Sometimes I ask intermediate-grade teachers, "What would happen if you walked into your class tomorrow and told your students to go write anything they want?" I usually hear one of two very different responses: "My students would say, 'What do you want me to write about? What genre do you want me to write in?'" Or "My students would say, 'Great! I have a zombie story / how-to-skateboard article / poem that I've been wanting to work on.'"

Clearly, the second version is the goal, but don't despair if your students respond like those in the first one. Units like this one and the others described here are the perfect antidote. If students who are used to being told what to write about and what genre to write in are given choices, their hidden ability to find their own writing projects can quickly emerge.

Interestingly, the first response doesn't tend to happen with younger children. I've never had a kindergartner on the first day of writing workshop ask me what they should write about or what genre to write in. I realize they don't yet know much about genres, so they might not think to ask this question. The point is that not knowing doesn't stop them from getting started, especially if we say very little about how to jump in. Kindergartners love to make things, so if we give them markers and paper, they will go make something.

But many older children do have trouble choosing a project and getting started. This unit teaches them how to create independent projects, both in this unit and throughout the year. In the intermediate grades, we want students to have independent writing projects throughout the year that they can always pull out of their folder to work on. Katie Wood Ray makes the case for this kind of "backup work" in *Study Driven* (2006). During the independent writing part of writing workshop, students should always be writing. If they think they are done, they could start a new piece for the unit they're working on, or they could put entries in their notebook. *Or* they could work on an independent project if they are in a genre study.

In a craft or process study, independent projects become the primary writing. For example, a fourth grader might have a fantasy story that was an independent project/backup piece during a feature article unit, but it becomes their primary piece when the class moves into a punctuation study.

→ **You might choose this study if . . .**

- *Your students don't know how to create their own writing projects.*

- *You want to maximize energy for writing right at the start of the year.*

- *You want students to have independent writing projects throughout the year.*

Grade Range

3–6. Any time students are in a craft or process study where they can determine their own genre, they will have to find writing projects to create. Students in the primary grades do this as they figure out the topic and genre for their next book. But when it's outside the context of a picture book, it can be more challenging for older students. Therefore, the focus of this unit is on supporting older students in finding genres and topics that create energy for writing.

Time of Year

This unit would typically be the first, or an early one, in the year so that students could benefit from having independent projects throughout the year, as their primary work in craft and process studies and as backup work in genre studies.

Student Learning and the Writing Celebration

During the celebration, students will share not only the project but how they decided on it. Why did they choose the genre? How did they find the topic? Whom are they writing for? They might write a short reflection and attach it to their writing. Or they might talk about their writing before they share it. Students might also share what their next project is going to be or a future project they want to tackle.

Students may have chosen to write something fairly long and may not be finished. Students could certainly share the portion they are most eager to show others or an unfinished piece that they started later in the unit after completing something else.

Since this unit will likely occur early in the year, this celebration might be fairly simple. Students should be particularly energized by what they have written, and most will be eager to share their writing with others. Other students, especially those who have taken a risk and tried something new, might be more hesitant to share. You might need a conversation before the celebration about how to respond to peers' writing in encouraging ways so that students will continue to be comfortable taking risks.

Key Unit Question

How did you decide on this topic, genre, audience, and purpose?

Gathering Published Mentor Texts

You will need a wide variety of published texts for this stack. It's important to show students lots of possibilities for what they might make, so I often pull a piece of writing from each of the other units in the year, as well as samples of other genres that are not represented. For example, I might include a fantasy short story in my stack even if we don't study fantasy short stories as a unit of study. Students often revert back to the last genre they remember studying or whichever genre they have studied most over the years. The stack should represent many of the different types of writing that students might decide to make, both in this unit and throughout the year. (Note that in a unit on studying your own stack of texts [Chapter 9], *students*, with your help, will gather their own stack based on a genre they want to study.)

This unit pulls from parts of other units to help students find ideas, plan, and revise, so you will also need samples of your own writing and student writing to show different processes for writing, beyond what they can see in finished, published pieces of writing. For example, you might need to show how you plan writing in different genres.

What Might I Teach?

Primary Goal

Students will independently create writing projects on topics of interest in genres of their choice.

Possible Teaching Points

What Do You Want to Make?

The following minilessons could be taught separately or combined:

- How do you find topics you care about?
- What are possible genres you might choose?
- Whom are you writing for? Where will your writing go when you're finished?
- What is your purpose for your piece of writing?
- How do you align topic, genre, audience, and purpose?

Planning

- Finding the right type of plan that will fit the genre you've chosen
- Exploring different planning strategies
- Trying out different types of plans

Drafting and Crafting

You might teach a few minilessons on improving the quality of writing. You'll have all year to work on improving writing, but a few lessons here will embed the idea that our goal is for students to become better writers. In these lessons you will want to show how a crafting technique cuts across genres. For example, you might show interesting word choice in a feature article, a fantasy short story, and a review to highlight how authors in any genre consider word choice.

You might also consider teaching into

- word choice;

- sentence variety;

- leads;

- endings.

Revision

Intermediate-grade students are sometimes reluctant to revise, so this unit provides an opportunity to positively influence students' disposition toward revision for the rest of the year. Any of the following teaching points would lay a foundation for revision.

- Why revision is important

- When to add to your writing

- When to take things out of your writing

- How to change big (structure) or small (word choice) parts of your writing

- How to try things out, knowing you can change them back

- How to revise without recopying: the logistics of revision

Editing

You might pick one or two things to work on related to conventions based on what you have seen from students early in this unit.

General Teaching Points

- How to say encouraging things during peer conferences and daily share times

- How to start your next piece, and your next, and your next

- How to choose what to share at the celebrations

Conferring

What to Carry with You

When conferring in this unit, I rely heavily on my own writing, including my own writer's notebook, and student writing, since many of the teaching points are related to the writing process. You will need to be able to show how you planned in various genres as well as show examples of revision in your own and student writing.

You'll definitely use the published pieces from a variety of genres that you've included in your stack in conferences, especially for students who are trying to figure out what they will make. You'll also need these published pieces to show students craft moves that authors make that they can try in their own writing.

When conferring, look for teaching points that are related to the unit goals, or that will help students write in any genre, before teaching something related to only the specific genre the child has chosen (as a last resort).

What to Think About While Conferring

As in other craft and process studies, you will want to first think about your goals for this unit. Does the child have an independent project? How is it progressing? Is the child engaged and self-directed?

When children are writing independently, we can use conferring to help them write *well*. Look for opportunities to tuck in process-oriented teaching points such as planning, revision, and editing, all of which will help them in other studies (including genre studies) throughout the year. You might also teach them about craft that cuts across genre, such as voice, punctuation, and word choice.

In Kohen's conference (Video 7.2), Kohen is writing an essay about why teenagers shouldn't work at McDonald's. I decide to teach him how to set composition goals that will improve the quality of his writing. I pull out two very different pieces of my own writing, a realistic fiction story and a feature article about tree houses. I then show him how I am thinking about my sentence variety in both pieces of writing. Sentence variety cuts across any genre, as does thinking about composition goals. And, intentionally, neither of the genres I showed was the same as his.

Video 7.2
Kohen's Conference

→ **For More on This Unit**

- *Independent Writing: One Teacher—Thirty-Two Needs, Topics, and Plans* by M. Colleen Cruz

- *Joy Write: Cultivating High-Impact, Low-Stakes Writing* by Ralph Fletcher

Chapter 8

Launching the *Use* of a Writer's Notebook

or

Using a Writer's Notebook as a Tool to Create Pieces of Writing

One October, Izzy was putting an entry in her writer's notebook, which she did three to four times each week. On this day she was writing about her trip to the sporting goods store that afternoon to buy running shorts. She wrote about how frustrated she was that they had only pink shorts. "Why does everyone think girls like pink?" she wrote, following up with a paragraph-long rant about how much she hates pink.

She captured the moment and the mood, felt better, and went on with her life, not thinking she would ever need that entry. It wasn't until four months later that she found out she needed that entry. Her fifth-grade class was studying persuasive essays, and one of the strategies they were using to find topics was to go back to their writer's notebook and reread their entries, looking for possible ideas to write about. Izzy found her entry about running shorts and used it as the basis for her essay about why you shouldn't make assumptions about people based on their gender.

Izzy used her notebook as a tool to create pieces of writing in much the same way that published authors use their notebooks: to collect entries, create plans, keep notes about writing, and try things out. It's the same way I use my writer's notebook, where I collect stories about my children and created plans for this book. And that's the goal of this unit! To help students use their notebooks authentically, in ways that will support their writing lives forever.

Rationale for the Study

In this unit students will learn how to use a writer's notebook. A writer's notebook is a tool to support the creation of pieces of writing. It's a place to capture moments and find ideas. It's also a place for rehearsal and trying things out.

The key to this unit is the idea of *using* a writer's notebook, rather than *keeping* a writer's notebook. We don't want students collecting ideas for the sake of collecting them. The notebook itself isn't the goal. Instead, they're collecting ideas knowing that they might use them someday in a piece of writing. When students are *keeping* a writer's notebook, it's more like a journal or diary, where students are just writing in the notebook but not revisiting the entries. A diary is not intended to be made public—you won't generally revisit diary entries with the intention of using them for another piece of writing. Diaries are wonderful, but the intention is different from how we teach students to use a writer's notebook.

Students will use their writer's notebooks throughout the year (and hopefully into the summer), which means they will fill a notebook or more in a year. That's different from putting a lot of entries in your notebook in September, a few in October, and then none the rest of the year. Students might even bring their notebooks with them to the following grade and reflect on how their use of their notebook has grown, rather than starting over with a new notebook each year. Also, if students are going to be writing in their notebooks frequently, they will need to have them with them outside writing workshop, including at home. It's helpful if schools have a consistent stance toward notebook use across the grades so that students are not "rediscovering" how a notebook should be used each year (Ray 2006).

Students can put lots of different things in their notebooks. Following are three common items teachers have students include:

- *Regular entries*: Students write a paragraph or two about something that happened, something they noticed, or something they wondered about; make lists of possible topics; and so on (see the books listed at the end of this chapter for lots of ideas on types of entries).

- *Planning and trying out*: Students might make a plan for a feature article or might try two different types of endings for an essay.

- *Notes*: Students might keep notes for a unit, for example, a list of the different types of leads they noticed when studying realistic fiction.

I don't have students draft in a writer's notebook since it's difficult to revise a draft in that context. When students are drafting, I want them to be able to do everything possible to revise without being dependent on recopying: taping a piece of paper to the side of a page, writing on the back, crossing out a line and writing above it, and so on. This can be hard in a notebook.

No matter how you envision your students' notebooks, students need to learn how to use them, if they haven't before. And the process will be more engaging when they choose what genre to write in.

→ **You might choose this study if . . .**

- *Your grade level is the first grade in your school where students use a writer's notebook as a tool for creating pieces of writing.*

- *Your students are used to using a notebook as more of a journal or a place for writing drafts, and you want to help them see how authors use writer's notebooks to create pieces of writing.*

- *You want your students to use their notebooks in a more meaningful way and want to strengthen the connection between notebooks and pieces of writing.*

Grade Range

3–6. I suggest launching the use of writer's notebooks in grade 3, but I know teachers who start using a modified writer's notebook halfway through grade 2.

A writer's notebook is a tool for creating pieces of writing, and since kindergarten and first-grade students are more "in the moment writers," the concept of putting ideas in a notebook for later use doesn't make as much sense.

Time of Year

This study would typically come at the beginning of the year if students have never used a writer's notebook before. Of course, it can also occur at whatever point in the year your students will start using a writer's notebook.

Student Learning and the Writing Celebration

For the celebration, choose something that allows students to show the connection between their notebooks and the writing they created. One possibility could be to have a gallery walk where students display their writing and have their writer's notebook open to the page that shows how they used it. Some examples could be

- the notebook page with the entry that inspired their writing;

- the page with the plan for their writing;

- a page where they tried out three different leads or a different ending;

- a page with a list of possible topics with the topic they chose highlighted.

What's key is that students can show how they've used a notebook to create a piece of writing so they can continue to do so throughout the year.

Key Unit Questions

How are you using your notebook to create your writing?
   or
What's working well for you in your notebook?
   or
How is your notebook helping you become a better writer?

These questions not only help students think about how they are using their notebooks but also provide teachers with important information about how the unit is going.

Finding Mentor Authors

This is one of the units where we don't start with a stack of texts. Instead of a collection of writing, we refer to what authors say about using writer's notebooks, blog tours of their notebooks, and video clips of authors talking about how they use writer's notebooks. Some links to get you started can be found at www.authortoauthor.org.

The most powerful mentor in this unit will be your own writer's notebook. It's one thing to hear what published authors say about their notebooks, but your notebook will be much more relevant and powerful for your students. It's also helpful to copy and save pages from student notebooks from year to year. I know students who have even donated or loaned their old notebooks so teachers can show what previous students have done. It is also powerful to invite former students back to show and talk about how they are using their notebooks in the next grade level.

What Might I Teach?

Primary Goals

Students will use a writer's notebook as a tool to publish pieces of writing.
    or
Students will use a writer's notebook, including putting entries in their notebooks throughout the year, to help them create pieces of writing.

Possible Teaching Points

In this unit, it makes sense to have students get started with a piece of writing very quickly so that they have something to work on as they learn how to use a writer's notebook. You'll teach them to use notebook entries to find additional ideas to write about, both in this unit and throughout the year.

Getting a Piece of Writing Started

You will have to decide whether to start with students just putting different types of entries in their notebooks or to start with students creating a piece of writing right away. You might have lessons on

- Finding topics

- Choosing a genre

- Using strategies for planning your writing in advance

Immersion/Initial Lesson

You might start with an initial lesson to set the stage for the unit by

- Looking at what authors say about writer's notebooks

- Showing what you put in your writer's notebook

- Showing notebooks from previous years

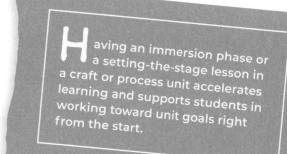

Having an immersion phase or a setting-the-stage lesson in a craft or process unit accelerates learning and supports students in working toward unit goals right from the start.

Expanding the Types of Notebook Entries Students Write

At first we just want students to get in the routine of putting any type of entry in their notebooks. But soon you will want to help students include a variety of types of entries. The books listed at the end of this chapter will give you numerous ideas for different types of entries. Here are just a few to get you going:

- Make lists of all kinds—things you love, beautiful words, and so on.

- Create heart maps (Heard 2016) to help find favorite topics and genres.

- Write about things you know a lot about.

- Write about big or little events that have happened to you.

- Write about small things you've noticed.

- Write about things that bug you or things you want to change.

- Write about times that you had a big feeling or about vivid memories.

- Make lists of questions (Fletcher 2003) and write about what you imagine some answers might be.

- Make sketches and drawings.

Using Student Notebooks to Plan and Try Things Out

Students can create plans for writing in their notebooks or use their notebooks to keep the plans they create in other places. It's also a place for trying things out, so you might have lessons on

- Using a notebook page to plan out your writing

- Sketching and writing about your characters (if you are writing a story, which is, of course, not required)

- Writing everything you can about a topic as a way of helping you think about what you know

- Trying a topic on for size to see if you know enough about it or enjoy writing about it

- Trying out a different beginning or ending for your piece of writing

Getting Student Writing Ready to Share

Students will create pieces of writing and choose a piece to share at the celebration. You might show students

- How to select a piece of writing to share at the publication

- How to do some final revision (they were hopefully also revising along the way)

- How to do some final editing

Conferring

What to Carry with You

In this unit, it will be crucial that you carry your own writer's notebook with you. It's very difficult to teach students to do something that we haven't done ourselves, so if students are going to use a notebook, you need to use a notebook. Sometimes teachers tell me that they don't have their own writer's notebook, and, of course, if you don't write outside school or aren't actively trying to publish pieces of writing, then you wouldn't have a notebook. Even if that's the case, teachers must have a writer's notebook to use as a teaching tool in the classroom.

For example, when you're showing students how to put different types of entries in their notebooks, it's important to be able to show a variety of entries in your notebook, even if you're generating those entries only as teaching tools. If you're teaching students how to try out different leads for a mystery story, you need to be able to show how you tried different leads for your mystery story in your notebook—even if you wouldn't really write a mystery story in your life outside teaching.

In Video 8.1: Jack's Conference, Jack is using his notebook in several ways throughout the year. He's using a list of topics he's been adding to all year. He also uses his notebook to plan pieces of writing and to keep notes about techniques the class has learned. In this conference, I decide to show Jack an additional use for his notebook. Jack is in an essay unit, but this skill can be used in any unit and would be introduced in a study on using a writer's notebook. Jack has finished his first essay and is starting to think about his next essay topic. He loves football and is thinking that his next essay might have something to do with football and friendships. I decide to show him how I use my notebook (Figure 8.1) to explore an idea by writing a stream of thoughts about the topic to see where it might lead. I show him how writing about tree houses in my notebook helped me remember events that I had forgotten about and think of new writing topics. Jack then tries it out by writing everything he can think of about football in his notebook to see where it leads him.

It is also extremely helpful to have on hand copies of pages of student notebooks from previous years. Students need to see what it looks like when a student tries something out in their notebook. If you don't have any examples now, it's not a problem, but save some this year to use in future years. And you *will* have student notebook examples quickly as your students start generating entries.

What to Think About While Conferring

Individual conferences allow us to see how students are taking what we're showing in the minilesson and applying those ideas in their notebook entries. As you confer, notice what types of entries students have been writing. Ask them how they have been using their notebooks. Listening to students talk

Figure 8.1   Matt's Notebook Page

Video 8.1

Jack's Conference

about their notebooks might lead you to teach them how to try out different types of entries or how to use their notebooks to plan or try something out.

If students' notebook work is going well, since this unit tends to be placed early in the year, you might focus on teaching crafting techniques or teaching points that will lay the foundation for skills they will use and develop throughout the year.

→ For More on This Unit

- *Breathing In, Breathing Out: Keeping a Writer's Notebook* by Ralph Fletcher

- *Independent Writing: One Teacher—Thirty-Two Needs, Topics, and Plans* by M. Colleen Cruz

- *Notebook Know-How: Strategies for the Writer's Notebook* by Aimee Buckner

- *A Writer's Notebook: Unlocking the Writer Within You* by Ralph Fletcher

Chapter 9

Independent Genre Study

or

Gathering and Studying Your Own Stack of Texts

Much of the thinking in this unit is based on the work, ideas, and conversations with writing and teaching expert Isoke Nia.

Fifth-grade teacher Kate started the year with a unit on finding and developing independent writing projects. Her students were highly engaged as they created writing on a variety of topics in a wide range of genres. She learned a lot about how they planned and revised, but she wasn't sure how well they could read like writers. As they progressed through the year with several genre studies, she discovered that her students were learning to notice what authors did in their writing but weren't consistently trying out what they noticed.

After the holiday break, Kate decided to start with a unit on independent genre studies. She started by asking students to talk about their favorite genres and choose one they wanted to study. Groups quickly formed around various genres: fantasy, feature articles, how-to articles, biographical sketches, poetry, and realistic fiction. She helped students find stacks of texts in the classroom and library. Some groups also found video clips of authors talking about their process for writing poetry and graphic short stories. Once the students had their stacks, Kate helped them apply what they already knew about reading like a writer and supported them in noticing more deeply. Her biggest emphasis was on students showing evidence of trying out techniques they had noticed. Every conference started with Kate asking, "What have you tried in your writing that you learned from the authors of your stack?"

Kate quickly noticed her students trying out techniques more often and intentionally than in the previous units. What's more significant is that students carried their improved noticing ability into their next genre study.

Rationale for the Study

In this unit students will strengthen their ability to read like writers by applying their ability to notice and try out in the genre of their choosing. This unit pulls together all the skills and techniques writers use to create pieces of writing. Rather than handing students a stack of texts based on a particular genre, we allow students in this unit to learn through collecting the mentor texts on which to base their writing. In the process, their understanding of the concept of genre will deepen—because they are determining a vision for what they will make, based on a stack of mentor texts they have chosen. The particular genre children choose doesn't matter. Since we will be teaching into the *process*, rather than the genre, the focus is on how to study *any* genre.

In many ways, this unit builds on and blends skills from other units in this book. It builds on Finding and Developing Independent Writing Projects (Chapter 7) by adding on the layer of students finding and studying their own stack of mentor texts, rather than using a teacher-chosen stack. It leans heavily on Reading Like a Writer (Chapter 5) since students will be noticing techniques in a stack of texts they found and trying these techniques out in their writing. And, of course, it borrows from Using Strategies to Find Topics (Chapter 6) and Genre Overview (Chapter 13) since students will be selecting topics and genre.

Your students needn't have encountered those studies before tackling the process of finding and studying their own stack. Regardless, it's important to be conscious of your particular students' experience with creating their own writing projects, reading like writers, and choosing topics and genres. When you have a deep sense of what your students need the most help with, you're more able to readjust the focus of your lessons and conferences to match.

In this unit students will often work in self-formed groups around a common interest. For example, you might have

- a group studying and writing graphic short stories;

- a group writing fiction or fantasy short stories;

- a group writing biographical sketches about athletes;

- a group writing informational feature articles;

- a group writing a mystery series in which all the stories have the same character.

However, you may also encounter students who aren't engaged by what other groups of children have chosen. Since I privilege student engagement over almost anything, if there is only one student who wants to write song lyrics, for example, I want that child to have the opportunity to do so.

→ **You might choose this study if . . .**

- *You want to see what your students truly understand about studying a genre and the writing process.*

- *You want to improve your students' ability to read like a writer in future genre studies.*

- *You want to increase students' engagement and agency and want to support their ability to independently tackle any type of writing they may encounter.*

Grade Range

3–6. Students in the primary grades certainly do study texts and create pieces of writing based on all sorts of writing they see in the world. But young children aren't typically finding their own stack of texts. Older students are more able to determine what stack they want to study, find that stack, and then create their own writing based on that stack.

Time of Year

This study could be placed at any point in the year. Earlier in the year, this unit increases writing engagement. Later in the year, students will be able to use what they've learned about studying stacks of texts and creating pieces of writing in other units as they work on independent writing projects.

Student Learning and the Writing Celebration

Students will be especially eager to share their writing due to the high level of ownership they have in this unit over both the process and the products they've created. Simply reading pieces of writing doesn't reveal the process the author went through.

Because process is such an important part of this study, you might choose a celebration that reveals and honors each student's process alongside what they've made. For example, students might have their stack of texts, lists of noticed techniques, plans, notebooks, and revisions on display with their writing. Or instead students might write a short reflection about what worked well and what was challenging about the process of creating this piece of writing.

Key Unit Questions

What characteristics have you noticed across your stack of texts that make it a genre?
   or
What are you doing in your writing that you have learned from your mentor?

Gathering Published Mentor Texts

Even though students will be finding stacks of mentor texts, the teacher still has a role in this process. You'll prepare by pulling all sorts of texts that students might be interested in—not just the typical texts we tend to study in school. In addition to fiction short stories, how-to articles, and poetry, you might pull graphic short stories (comics). Much of what you show students will be to help them broaden the range of what they might choose. We're also not expecting students to form stacks from only what's in the classroom. We want students to be searching for texts outside school as well. Therefore, teachers have to strike a tricky balance of making sure students have access to lots of different texts without inadvertently communicating that students can pull only from what's in the school.

For minilessons and conferences, you will need your own stack and pieces of writing to teach with. There are several options to consider:

- You might choose a genre to study yourself that is different from the ones students choose so that when you're conferring and teaching minilessons you're modeling in a different genre from what they're writing.

- You might rotate the stack you use in minilessons from day to day. On Monday you might model noticing word choice with one group's genre and show how you are trying it out in your genre. On Tuesday you might use a different group's stack, and so on.

- You might have a couple of genres of your own writing that are the same genre as students have chosen so that you can show how to notice and try something in different genres. In this case, you just have to be careful to make sure you don't make the teaching genre specific.

You will also want to make sure of the following:

- *Students are studying writing.* This sounds obvious, but in world of video, students often want to write something that ends up in a visual form—a Ted Talk, a speech, or a how-to video, for example. To make this work, it's important for students to study transcripts as well as video.

- *The chosen genre helps students become better writers and is worthy of deep study.* Again, this sounds obvious, but students might want to choose a genre they could indeed find a stack for that isn't rich enough in terms of craft. For example, baseball cards. You can collect a stack, and the writing on baseball cards could potentially be considered a genre—but listing statistics and a sentence or two about the featured athlete won't stretch students as writers.

- *Students are able to collect a stack of texts that represent the thing they are going to make.* If a child is going to study and write fantasy short stories, rather than a fantasy novel, then their stack should consist of fantasy short stories.

What Might I Teach?

Primary Goal

Students will create pieces of writing based on a stack of texts they each self-select and study.

Possible Teaching Points

Immersion

Rather than simply immersing students in a stack of texts, the immersion phase of this study is about immersing students in a wide variety of genres and topics to spark a variety of ideas for what they want to make. It's also helpful to encourage students to consider genres and projects that we might not have on hand in the classroom.

On the initial day of this study, make sure students have a clear understanding that the goal for this unit is for each student to independently undertake everything writers do to figure out how to create a piece of writing, which will allow them to independently tackle any type of writing they encounter, in or out of school. So we might also look at what published authors say about finding mentors and being inspired by pieces of writing.

Another way to start this unit is to have students quickly select genres they already know. After you help students gather a stack of genre-specific texts, they can then start to immerse themselves in their chosen genres.

Whether you help students decide on genres to study more in depth, or have students choose genres quickly, students will need time to simply read and study their genre.

Finding and Studying Mentor Texts

The early part of this unit will focus on supporting each student in finding and studying their own stack of texts. Teaching points for minilessons might include

- What types of things are you interested in making? Where have you seen this type of writing?

- How do you choose what to make?

- How to find texts in and out of school

- What makes a good mentor text? Consider length, style, topic, and craft

- How to notice key, defining characteristics of your genre

- How to notice techniques: Which techniques show up in all of your texts, most of your texts, or some of your texts?

- How to notice more sophisticated or subtle techniques

- How to make your own anchor chart

- How to show evidence of trying out what you've noticed in your stack

- How to do a close study of your stack: noticing specific craft/techniques

  - word choice

  - sentence variety

  - beginnings

  - endings

  - punctuation

  - interesting language

  - techniques to engage the reader

  - layout

  - figurative language

- How to use anchor charts from earlier in the year to find categories of techniques to notice

Developing Writing

As students begin to develop their writing, you can draw from some of the lessons that show up in other units in this book, such as

- Using what you have learned from your author in your writing (Chapter 5)

- Intentionally using techniques and articulating why you used the technique (Chapter 5)

- Selecting a planning structure that fits your genre (Chapter 10)

- Using your plan throughout your writing (Chapter 10)

- Conferring with peers (Chapter 11)

- Revising your writing as you go (Chapter 12)

The lessons your students need will vary depending on your class' strengths and needs. One year your class may need more support with planning, while another year it might need more support revising. You will also want to consider which other craft and process studies you have coming up, or have already had, in your year. If you've already had a revision study, for example, you would gear your lessons to reinforcing or extending the revision strategies they have already learned.

Conferring

What to Carry with You

You will need all three tools with you when you confer: published writing, your own writing, and student writing. As in all the units, it doesn't matter which genre you choose to study yourself, but you will need to be able to show how you've tried out a variety of techniques in that genre.

> In craft and process studies we're not teaching into any specific genre, so showing a technique in a genre different from what the child is writing in helps the child understand that the same technique can be used in more than one genre.

When you're conferring, it's important to show examples of how you are noticing techniques in your own stack and how you then use those techniques in your own writing. You could also use the student's stack to help them notice techniques the author is using and then teach into how to transfer what they're learning into their own writing.

You should be able to use your own stack or a student's stack since what you are teaching isn't related to a specific genre. Anything you are teaching could be taught with any genre.

What to Think About While Conferring

In this unit, because students are studying within particular genres, it is especially easy to fall into the trap of conferring specifically into the genre they've chosen. Keeping in mind that the goal is to help students choose and study *any* genre helps focus your teaching on process. When you teach into the process, you help students understand their particular genre without needing to be an expert in each genre being written in your classroom. The point is for students themselves to become experts (or expert-ish) in their genre.

To start most conferences, you can ask students to talk about what they have been noticing in their stack and what they have tried out in their writing. You might ask to see students' lists of noticed techniques. You might ask students what techniques they are thinking of trying next.

Once you see what they are already doing and what they are planning to do, then you can decide how to help them grow as a writer. You might decide to teach them any of the teaching points listed earlier:

- How to notice more in their stack

- How to notice more hidden techniques

- How to decide where to try out a technique

- How to try a technique and see how it feels before deciding whether to keep it (risk taking)

For More on This Unit

- *Independent Writing: One Teacher—Thirty-Two Needs, Topics, and Plans* by M. Colleen Cruz

- *Wondrous Words: Writers and Writing in the Elementary Classroom* by Katie Wood Ray

Chapter 10

Planning

or

Thinking Ahead in Any Unit of Study

or

Creating and Using Plans

No matter the genre, no matter the length, writers think ahead. As with all units discussed here, when students are able to write what and how they want, not only does energy for the unit go up, but the writing work also becomes more meaningful. Riley is a perfect example.

"Have you read the series Twilight?" Riley asked at the start of our conference (Video 10.1). It wasn't the question I was expecting to hear, but her passion was evident—note her disgust that the main character, Bella, "assumes everyone fixes her problems for her." Knowing Riley's inspiration helps me understand the novel she's writing, *The Great Murder Society*. Her goal is 5,000 words, and at the time of this conference she's up to 1,700—not actually novel length, but certainly much longer than what students might normally write in school. It makes sense that she sees Twilight as a mentor text. And how wonderful that the writing she's passionate about is valued at school and by her teacher!

Just as with topics like rap and Pokémon, I know barely enough to get by, topic-wise, in this conference. Fortunately, I don't need to know about a topic in order to be able to teach a student about being a better writer. I decide to teach Riley how to plan out a long piece of writing. She has such energy for this piece, and I don't want planning to decrease her energy, but the bigger a piece of writing is, the easier it is to get lost along the way—and even more so with fiction writing. Teaching into planning makes sense for this reason, and also because it's the focus of a planning unit.

I decide to show her how I plan for a large piece of writing, an informational article about tree houses. Since the teaching point is about thinking ahead in your writing in any genre, I don't need to have the same genre she's writing in. I have a fiction story I could have used, but it was a short story. I went with the tree house article because the length was more similar to that of Riley's piece.

After I show her how I'm planning my writing, I ask her if she is more of a boxes scene planner, or a list planner, or a web planner. My goal is for her to plan, and since her writing isn't part of a genre study, it's not about how to plan a fiction story—it's about the planning process. Riley shows me she understands this when she says, "I'm more of a bullet planner." Having an identity of yourself as a certain type of planner is one part of having a writing identity.

Video 10.1
Riley's Conference

Rationale for the Study

In this unit students will explore the idea of planning, learn how to align planning with a genre, and learn how to use their plan throughout a piece of writing. I often hear from intermediate-grade teachers that although they teach students how to plan and think ahead in their writing, students don't tend to make the transfer into planning their writing independently—often because they don't enjoy planning. They see it as a step (or hoop) to go through, rather than as a valuable tool.

You could (and should) certainly tackle these issues in genre studies throughout the year by including some minilessons on structure, planning, and organization. But a unit devoted to the idea of the importance of planning, and using plans in writing, allows students to better understand how thinking ahead strengthens their writing.

In order to do this, of course, students will have to actually plan and create pieces of writing. Practicing making plans that don't lead to actual pieces of writing would be like planning for a trip that you never take. Unless you take the trip, you won't know how well you planned and, subsequently, how to plan better in the future.

It's also important to make sure you use choice of genre (and topic) to energize writing in this unit. If you've chosen this unit because your students have low levels of energy for planning, ensuring they are able to choose genres and topics they care about will increase their engagement in a unit they might not otherwise be excited about. During this unit students will come to see patterns, commonalities, and differences in planning across genres. It's more difficult to compare planning strategies across an entire year than it is to compare planning across genres within a single unit.

Your own writing and planning process will be a great source for teaching points in this unit. If you haven't planned pieces of your own writing, you will want to plan and create a few pieces of writing in different genres to help you reflect on your own planning process.

→ **You might choose this study if . . .**

- *Your students don't see the purpose of planning or see planning as something they "have to do."*

- *Your students create plans for their writing but don't actively use their plans throughout the writing process.*

- *You want to help each student understand what type of planning is most beneficial for them and how planning could vary from genre to genre.*

- *You want students to engage in more efficient and meaningful planning in genre studies.*

Grade Range

3–6. In grades 3–6, students are ready to take on writing work that involves more extensive planning. We do, of course, teach K–2 students to think ahead in their writing, and as students become more sophisticated, their planning becomes slightly more involved and separate from their writing. I'd save this unit for grades 3–6, when students are using more complex plans and/or planning in a writer's notebook.

Time of Year

This unit could be placed at any point in the year. When it's placed earlier in the year, students can use and practice what they've learned about planning throughout the year. When it's placed later in the year, students can pull from their experiences planning in each of their earlier units.

Student Learning and the Writing Celebration

For this writing celebration students will share a finished piece of writing along with their plan. You might have a celebration that is more of a gallery walk where students show both their plans and pieces of writing. Or students might write reflections about how their plans did or didn't help their writing. Or the class might make a list of planning principles based on everyone's reflections that they can revisit in every unit throughout the year. And, of course, we will want students to have opportunities to read or share their writing with others.

Key Unit Question

How are you using your plan to support your writing?

This question assumes students are planning and focuses on how they are using their plan.

Finding Mentor Authors

When we study published texts, we can see the result of an author's planning, but we can't see what the author did before they started. Therefore, for this study we will have to look at what authors *say* about the importance of planning and about their own planning process, as well as their suggestions for planning. To get you started, you can find video clips online of authors talking about planning at www.authortoauthor.org.

You can find some authors' actual plans online also. A quick search for "J. K. Rowling plans" turns up several of her actual plans for the Harry Potter books.

While *her* plan won't help students plan their much shorter pieces of writing, seeing that real authors make real plans does help reinforce the idea that writers think ahead. And complex plans for novels have many of the same general characteristics (showing sequence, showing parts, showing connections) as plans students create.

You will also want to collect some of your own plans as well as student plans. Hopefully you saved some plans and notebooks from last year's students, but if not, invite former students back to your class to share their current plans.

What Might I Teach?

Primary Goals

Students will understand the importance of planning their writing and will plan more effectively.

or

Students will independently choose to plan writing throughout the year.

The second goal is a long-term goal, and to fully assess it, we'll have to look at student disposition toward planning at the end of the year, not just at the end of this unit. Having long-term goals helps us focus on crucial skills, such as children's disposition toward planning, beyond just their ability to plan in a certain genre or at a certain time of year.

Possible Teaching Points

As with many other units, your fellow grade-level teachers can be a huge support. As a grade level, you might decide to write in different genres on different topics with different plans, and then copy and share your plans across the team. Recently I was working with a group of teachers who were all starting a piece of writing. We gave teachers time to plan and then did a gallery walk where we could see everyone's plans. The range of planning styles and methods was diverse, with no two teachers planning exactly the same way. Looking at these plans quickly expanded our teaching possibilities.

Your own writing and planning process will be a great source for teaching points in this unit. If you haven't planned pieces of your own writing in a wide range of genres, it would be helpful to do so before the unit starts. How do you plan fiction stories? How do you plan how-to articles? Rather than studying a stack of texts, you and your grade-level team might spend time planning in different genres and then analyzing and sharing the strategies you used for planning. This exercise will yield more teaching points than days available!

You might also encourage students to choose relatively short pieces of writing so that they have the opportunity to plan more than once. We don't want students to just practice planning without then using their plan. Instead, we want them to gain experience creating and using plans, ideally more than once.

Setting the Stage

Students will benefit from a day at the beginning of the unit that sets the stage. You might start by watching several videos from your stack of clips of authors talking about their planning processes. You might do a gallery walk of all the teacher and student plans you have collected. You might interview older students about their planning processes.

You will also want to get a feel for where your students are already with planning and honor any frustrations they might have. Students could share

- their dispositions toward planning their writing;

- thoughts about where planning has helped;

- thoughts about why planning might be frustrating;

- how it helps when they plan ahead in other areas of life;

- how they feel when they're well prepared;

- what is challenging about planning.

You'll also share your own experiences with planning. It will be helpful if you are able to share several plans for pieces of writing that you have created in previous units over the years. You might also reflect on your own feelings about planning writing, both as a student and as an adult.

It's helpful to encourage students to decide what they are going to create early in this unit, so they have a project to start planning as soon as possible.

Creating Plans

- What are all of the different tools you can use to plan (webs, outlines, story maps, etc.)?

- How do people plan differently in different genres?

- What planning structure do you need for your genre?

In any craft or process study, you might need minilessons on choosing genres and choosing topics. If your students are choosing a narrow range of genres, a minilesson or two on choosing genres and picking a genre to go with a specific topic will help ensure students are choosing a genre rather than reverting back to what they have written most recently.

- How do you match your plan to the scope of your piece of writing?
- How do you modify a preset graphic organizer?
- What are common characteristics of plans?

Using Your Plan

- How to check in with your plan each day
- How to go back to your plan to help you figure out what's next
- How your plan might change across a piece of writing
- Why you should record changes on your plan
- How to use peer conferences to help you think about your plan

As in any unit, any of these teaching points might be taught in a single minilesson or across multiple minilessons.

Conferring

What to Carry with You

Your own planning tools, whether this means plans in your notebook or a stack of your own graphic organizers, or something else, will be an invaluable tool as you confer with students. You understand your own plans better than you understand published authors' plans or students' plans. This will be the easiest tool to teach with because you have insider information about why you chose to plan that way.

You will also need student plans, whether this means copies of plans from students' writer's notebooks or copies of graphic organizers from students from previous years. Like always, don't worry if you haven't saved any plans from previous years. If this isn't your first unit of the year, start saving plans in each of the units leading up to this unit. If this is your first unit of the year, you can start using the plans that students create (and save some for next year).

> Using a student in the class as a mentor in a conference with another student lifts the mentor student's status as a writer in the class and boosts their confidence.

What to Think About While Conferring

Remember that in this unit we are focusing on planning and using plans. Therefore, teaching into a student's individual genre choice won't work toward the goals for this unit and should be saved for last in your list of things to confer into.

The first thing to look at is how students are creating plans. Do they have a plan? How complex is it? How much has the writer modified or adjusted their plan to fit the project?

Once students have plans, you will want to see if they show evidence of actually using them. When you sit down next to a student, notice whether they have their plan out while they're writing. That sounds simple, but often when I sit down next to students, they don't have their plans out. More often, when I ask about their plan, students start searching through their folder or desk, basically saying, "I know I have it in here somewhere." It's hard to use it if you don't have it. If students have their plan out, then ask how they are using it. Ask, "Is your plan helpful? What has changed in your plan since you started writing?" Often these questions will lead to teaching points.

When I ask Brennan in his conference (Video 10.2) if he's planned his writing out, he says he's been thinking about it. "My plan is in my head" is a common reply. Showing him how another student plans might make planning seem both more achievable and more concrete, so I bring Amoura over to show how she's planning her story. It doesn't matter that she's planning a story and he's writing an informational article—my teaching point is about planning and thinking ahead, and Amoura's plan is a great example.

In Eli's conference (Video 10.3), I go for a more specific aspect of planning. I decide to show him how to think about the scope of his writing—in particular, where to start and stop. To help Eli think about this in his baseball

Video 10.2
Brennan's Conference

Video 10.3
Eli's Conference

Video 10.4
Amoura's Conference

story, I bring Gianna over to show how she's narrowing down the scope of her Neil Armstrong historical fiction.

In Amoura's conference (Video 10.4), I use myself as the mentor. I show her how I use different structures to plan in different genres, and then I ask her to figure out how she wants to plan her story. You can see her plan in Figure 10.1.

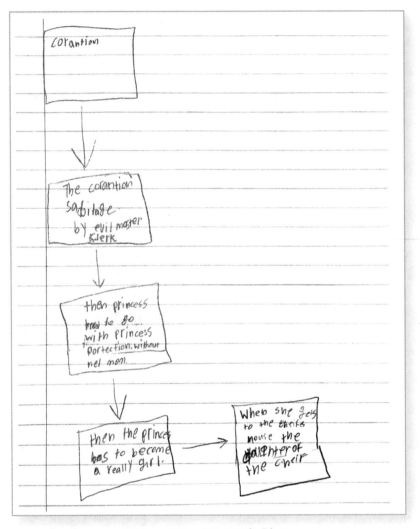

Figure 10.1   Amoura's Plan

Thank you to Corinne Arens and the teachers in Blue Springs, Missouri, for initially thinking about this unit.

Chapter 11

How to Have Better Peer Conferences

or

How to Have Better Conversations About Your Writing with Teachers and Peers

or

Using Conversation to Improve Writing

C hristin Forbes wanted to teach her fifth-grade writers to have more effective conversations with a unit on how to have better peer conferences. Christin had noticed that students were asking what their partner thought of their writing in general, rather than asking for support in a specific part. We decided to teach students how to think about a specific part of their writing they would like their partner to look at, and ask for support in that area. In Video 11.1: Minilesson on Peer Conferring, I start by modeling a peer conference with Ethan, asking him whether he thinks the beginning of my realistic fiction story is too long. After he tells me it seems about right, he points out a part at the end of the story that he thought was confusing.

After seeing me model what asking for help in a specific spot in your writing sounds like, Cameron and Lola try this out in front of the class. It's important to show what it sounds like when *students* try out this skill. Cameron asks for help with description, and Lola asks for help with her ending. While they're giving each other advice, I point out for the class some of the moves they're making.

The skills that make up effective conversations aren't easy to see, so we want to make them explicit, without making them sound scripted. By making the invisible visible in minilessons and conferences, we help students become aware of what they can do so they can consistently and independently have conversations that affect their writing—no matter the genre.

Rationale for the Study

Video 11.1

Minilesson on Peer Conferring

In this unit students will learn how to use specific strategies to make their conversations about writing more effective. Most teachers hope that students will be able to talk about their writing with more sophistication in May than in September. But unless teachers actively support children's growth in this area, not much tends to change.

While we want students to get better at talking with peers about their writing, we also want their writing conversations with teachers to get richer throughout the year. When we ask open-ended questions at the beginning of the year, we're not surprised when we hear simple answers. When we say, "What are you trying to get better at in your writing?" we're not surprised when a student says, "Umm . . . spelling." But by the end of the year, we expect students to be more articulate and reflective as they talk about their writing.

In every unit throughout a year, you might include a peer conferring goal. If you teach into peer conferring in this way, students should get incrementally better at talking about their writing with each unit. I wouldn't include a peer conferring unit in every grade. But, by including a full unit on talking with others about your writing in *some grades*, you can jump-start and accelerate students' conversation growth. Students will be much better at talking about their writing, more quickly, if that's what you focus on for several weeks.

→ **You might choose this study if . . .**

- *Your students aren't currently having peer conferences and you would like them to start having peer conferences.*

- *Your students are having peer conferences and you would like them to have better conversations more quickly.*

- *You'd like to raise the level of sophistication of student talk with peers and their teacher.*

- *Your students think of peer conferring only as peer editing.*

The goal of this unit is not for children to actually get great writing advice from a partner. They might, but that's not the expectation. Nor is the goal for students to master conferring. Conferring is challenging even for us as teachers, so we should not expect students to "out-confer" us. Instead, the benefits of this unit stem from children seeing their writing through someone else's eyes, considering another perspective, explaining what they are doing as a writer, and talking with someone about their writing.

Grade Range

K–6. Student conversations about writing will sound very different in kindergarten than in sixth grade, but at any age the goal is for students to get better at having meaningful conversations about their writing. Kindergartners might suggest adding something to an illustration, while sixth graders might help a peer rethink their structure.

Time of Year

This unit could take place at any time of year, but if it's earlier in the year, students will be set up to have meaningful conversations about writing all year long. This is usually a three- to four-week unit and could be easily placed between two longer genre studies.

Student Learning and the Writing Celebration

Throughout this unit, we expect students to have more meaningful conversations that affect their writing. At the writing celebration, students will show places in their writing where a conversation with a peer influenced it. Students might show a revision they made based on a conversation. They might share how a conversation with a partner reinforced what they already were thinking about their writing and gave them the confidence to keep it as it was. Of course, what they share will be very different based on grade level, but at any age we're looking for evidence, big or small, of a connection between conversation and writing.

Key Unit Questions

Most conferences in this unit start with me listening into a peer conference and noticing what the students' conversation sounds like. If I was going to interrupt and ask a question, it might be

What are the two of you doing to have better conversations?

or

How are your conversations changing over time?

During this unit teachers will also confer with individual students. In those conferences, the first question could be

How has a conversation with your partner helped this piece of writing?

or

What part of your writing has been influenced by a conversation with a classmate?

Finding Mentor Authors

For this unit, we can't see how published texts were influenced by the conversations authors had with other people. Published authors do talk frequently with people about their writing, especially with their editors. Different authors have different relationships with their editors. Instead of texts, we will use video clips of authors sharing how talking with others supports their writing. For clips of authors talking about how talk benefits their writing, go to www.authortoauthor.org.

What Might I Teach?

Primary Goals

Students will have better conversations about their writing.

or

Students will articulate how talking with their teacher and their partner has influenced their writing.

Finding Teaching Points in a Peer Conferring Unit

The best way to find teaching points for this unit is to have some peer conferences yourself and then analyze what made your conversation go well. When I project this unit with teachers, we start by sharing a bit of our own writing (sometimes starting a piece on the spot) with another teacher. After taking turns conferring with each other, we list what went well. The list always grows quickly!

It can also be helpful to watch students conferring with each other, and then discuss later what we would like them to do better. We don't expect them to be skilled at talking about their writing—even adults often struggle with this. By listening to students talk with their partners, we can easily envision what would help their conversations be just a bit more effective.

Peer Conferring Logistics

With Whom Will Students Confer?

I usually assign writing partners for peer conferences based on what I know of each of the students. For example, I wouldn't pair the chattiest child with the quietest, and I wouldn't pair the two most talkative children, and so on. The advantage of having a set partner is that conversations go better when you are talking with someone you feel comfortable with. It's much easier for me to take risks in sharing my writing with my friend and editor Zoë because I know she will be thoughtful with her advice. Having a set partner also ensures that everyone is getting the same amount of practice conferring. When students choose whom to confer with day by day, some students may not get enough practice conferring if they aren't frequently chosen to confer with.

Some teachers have students choose a partner to confer with. Figure 11.1 shows a class chart of children's self-described writing strengths, which students use to choose a partner to confer with based on need. This helps students see everyone as having areas of specialty and allows them to develop their conferring skills with more than one student. In this case, you just need to be mindful that everyone is having opportunities to confer.

Another possibility could be for students to confer with one assigned partner early in the unit to develop their skills, and then choose another partner to confer with at the end of the unit so that the skills they've developed transfer to whomever they are talking with. Regardless of whom they are conferring with, the same key ideas about peer conferring will apply. Figure 11.2 shows one class' reminders about when to confer and with whom to confer.

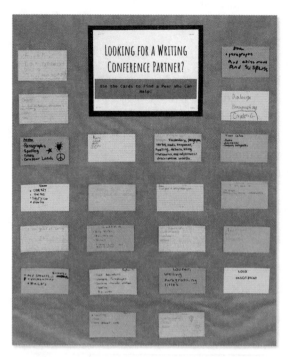

Figure 11.1 "Looking for a Writing Conference Partner?"

PeeR CoNfeReNciNG

When? • rough draft is finished
• stuck on where to go next
• suggestions on revision
• choosing a topic or genre
• need opinions / reassurance
• proofreading final copies
• editing
• after a few pages
• check tone or on-topic
• check to see if message is clear
• requirements of genre

Who? *CONSTRUCTIVE CRITICISM
• someone who gives
• a good writer that can help you grow
• a person you can FOCUS with
• someone who stays on task and follows rules
• compatible partner
• different strengths
• willing partner

Figure 11.2 Supporting Student Conferring Partner Choice: When and Who

When to Have Peer Conferences?

There are several ways you might structure the timing of peer conferences:

- *Point in time:* Students might have peer conferences at certain points in the week. You might say, "Today is Wednesday, so have a peer conference before you start writing today." This ensures everyone has regular conferences.

- *Point in the process:* Some teachers have students confer at a point in the process. You might say, "Have a peer conference before you plan your writing."

- *As needed:* The most natural structure would be to have a peer conference when you need one. While this avoids forced conversations, it might cause some students to have numerous peer conferences and other students to have few, if any. In this unit we want to ensure all students have equal opportunities to talk about their writing.

Ultimately, you might decide to use a combination of these structures.

Possible Teaching Points

Setting the Stage

In this unit we aren't immersing students in texts; we are immersing them in thinking about having better conversations. Hopefully students have already had peer conferences at some point in their writing lives at school. On the unit's initial day, we might talk about

- What makes a good conversation?

- How can you tell when someone isn't listening to you?

- How do you feel when someone says something unkind?

- How can you tell when someone says something they don't mean?

On this day we can also share what published authors say about talking with others about their writing.

Peer Conferences

There are a lot of things for students to consider while learning how to talk about their writing (see Figure 11.3 for conferring reminders in a fifth-grade class). To try to improve students' strategies in peer conferences, here are some teaching points you might offer them in minilessons and conferences:

- Sit next to each other and look at just one person's writing.

- Think about what to say at the start or end of a conference.

- Decide on a good location to have a conference.

- Decide when to have a peer conference.

- Ask for help in a certain part of your writing (see Video 11.1). Think about what you need to do to prepare for a peer conference.

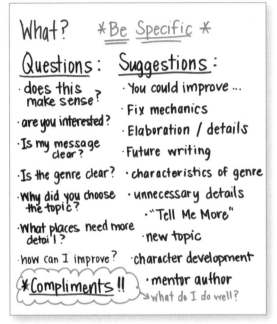

Figure 11.3 Peer Conferring Questions and Suggestions

- Decide if your partner should read the whole piece of writing or just a section.

- Say kind things during a peer conference.

- Say *specific* kind things during a peer conference.

- Give your partner advice. (At first, we as teachers go for any kind of advice, knowing it will likely be very general. For example, "You could add more detail.")

- Give your partner specific advice. Advice becomes more helpful when it is more specific. For example, "You could add dialogue in this part of your story."

- Consider whether to take your partner's advice.

- Ask clarifying questions.
- Have back-and-forth conversations.
- Try out your partner's advice to see if you like it.
- Show your partner how you tried something in your writing.
- Suggest your partner try out a technique from an anchor chart.
- Select a strategy for what to do if you're not sure what to say in a peer conference.
- Give advice about composition, rather than about conventions.
- Use resources such as anchor charts in the classroom to figure out what to say.
- Remember and use strategies for being a good listener.
- Have a better range of suggestions (techniques).
- Paraphrase for understanding.
- Talk with your partner about your process, not just your product.
- Ask your partner if your writing is clear (or engaging).
- Share your goal for your writing and ask if your partner thinks you have met your goal.

Talking with Your Teacher

You might consider a series of lessons focused on examining a student's role in a conference. We want children to see that they are partial owners of a conference and that actively talking will help them learn more. Some of the topics we might teach are

- How to answer Carl Anderson's (2000) question "How's it going?"
- How to talk about what you are doing well in your writing
- How to talk about what you are working on in your writing
- Saying more about your writing
- Saying more specific things about your writing

Conferring

It's easy, when we have minilessons on peer conferring, to forget to confer into peer conferences. It's even easier, when conferring into peer conferences, to forget to teach into the peer conferring itself. Conferences provide a wonderful opportunity to strengthen students' conversations in meaningful ways.

What to Carry with You

When conferring, you will have two tools you can teach with. You can show a student partnership what you (yourself) did during a peer conference or what your partner did or said that worked well. Or instead, you can show what another student partnership did in their peer conference. Using one of these tools will help you make sure you are modeling and showing what good conversations look like, rather than just describing them.

When projecting any unit, it's good to plan for more teaching possibilities than days available. It's helpful to have extra ideas on hand when you decide you need a different lesson from what you had projected, based on what your students need in general. This will also give you a broader range of conference teaching points, which will help you meet diverse individual needs.

What to Think About While Conferring

Your conferences will often start with listening in for a minute or two, rather than with a question. Next, think about what these students could do to have a more effective conversation. If you are stuck for a teaching point, you might ask the partnership what they have been working on in their conversations and what you could do to help them. If they don't know, then you have discovered a teaching point: how to set goals for conversations. We want students to see that while some conversations just naturally go well based on chemistry, there are characteristics of good conversations that can be practiced.

You might also confer about how to have a better conversation with you. Reflect on what the child has done previously in conferences with you, and be explicit about what you would like to do next. For example, you might start a conference by saying, "I've noticed that when we talk about your writing you have been listening carefully and trying out what we talk about. Today I want to show you how to say more about your writing" (or whatever your teaching point is).

→ For More on This Unit

* *How's It Going? A Practical Guide to Conferring with Student Writers* by Carl Anderson

* *Independent Writing: One Teacher—Thirty-Two Needs, Topics, and Plans* by M. Colleen Cruz

* *A Teacher's Guide to Writing Conferences* by Carl Anderson

Chapter 12

Revision

or

Improving Children's Disposition Toward Revision

or

Supporting Children's Skills in Adding, Deleting, Moving, and Changing Their Writing

Learning to thoughtfully revise, in any genre, is one of the most important and useful writing skills and dispositions of all. We want to teach students that revision does not mean recopying or redoing their writing, or simply editing for spelling, punctuation, and grammar. Instead, revision is part of the creative process—it's about playing around with writing and trying things out, rather than making it "right."

In Video 12.1: Minilesson on Revision, I am focusing on the strategy of *taking things out*. It's completely authentic—I really do have a hard time taking things out of my writing. Many students do also, especially if it was difficult to get the words on the page in the first place. When I'm showing students how and why to take something out, I emphasize that it doesn't have to stay out. I don't erase it. Instead, I take it out temporarily, knowing that I can put it back in. As one student says, "You don't have to burn it. It could be like your backup on the side if you decide to do it for real."

I'm also trying to position revision as something *all authors do*. When Harper describes taking something out in her writing, I say, "I'm thinking I could be like Harper," and then I actually take a paragraph out of my writing.

Rationale for the Study

In this unit you will nurture children's ability to revise their writing independently. Young children, especially kindergartners (and preschoolers even more so), are quick to revise. If there is a marker nearby when a young child is rereading their book, they are likely to add to their illustrations or text. So, in the primary grades, this unit is focused more on being intentional about revision decisions and expanding revision beyond adding on (children's most common form of revision) to also include the process of changing and taking out.

In the intermediate grades, we often see children who are reluctant to revise. Sometimes they associate revising with recopying, which would make anyone hesitant to revise. It's important that we separate revision (the act of adding, deleting, moving, or changing) from recopying (making writing look nice). We want to make sure students don't think you have

Video 12.1

Minilesson on Revision

to recopy something in order to be able to add to it, or delete something, or move a part, or make a change.

We also need to make sure that students don't see revision as something they get ready to do only before they share (publish) a piece of writing. We need to support students in revising both as they write and as they revisit a piece while they are working on it. Too often, students see revision only as one phase of the writing process, rather than as an ongoing process.

→ **A Few Quick Informal Definitions**

- *Revising:* Improving the quality of writing by adding, deleting, changing, or moving.

- *Editing:* Making the conventions of writing (spelling, grammar, punctuation) more correct.

- *Publishing:* The act of making writing public in some way by sharing it with the world. Writing doesn't have to be recopied, edited, or revised in order to share it, and writing isn't published until it is shared.

- *Recopying:* Rewriting a piece of writing to make it easier to read.

Grade Range

K–6. While a revision study would be beneficial in any grade, this unit can be especially powerful in grades 4–6, when some students become more reluctant to revise.

Time of Year

This unit could be placed at any point in the year. In the primary grades I might place it later in the year when students have more writing to look back on, while in the upper grades I might place it earlier in the year so that it would influence students' disposition toward revision throughout the remainder of the year.

→ **You might choose this study if . . .**

- *Your students are reluctant to revise.*

- *You want children to think more deeply about their writing.*

- *You want to support your students' ability to improve the quality of their writing.*

- *You want to support a mindset of reflection and help students look at their writing through a strength-based lens.*

Student Learning and the Writing Celebration

Throughout this unit you'll notice increased evidence of intentionality in students' revisions, as well as strengthened ability to talk about their revision decisions. During the writing celebration we will want to highlight revision decisions students made. We might also want students to reflect on how their disposition toward revision changed throughout the unit. When students are sharing their writing, they will also explain one or two specific revisions they made and why they made them. If the celebration is a gallery walk, students can have sticky notes on their writing showing revisions they made. Older students might show a draft and their final product to show the actual revisions they made.

Key Unit Questions

What revisions have you made in your writing?
     or
Which is the most effective revision decision you have made as an author?
     or
What have you done well in your writing?

Poetry Studies in Service of Revision

One way to improve children's revision skills at any age is through a poetry study. Because poems tend to be relatively short, it's easy for children to play around with revision. They can take things out and move things around. They can revise for line breaks (when studying poems that don't rhyme) and layout to work on how poems sound. It's a great unit for working on revising for word choice (especially when studying poems that don't rhyme). Unfortunately, I see fewer and fewer poetry units in schools I work in. Be sure to look at your schools' units across grades to see where poetry units are placed. For more about poetry study and how it affects other types of writing, read *Poems Are Teachers* by Amy Ludwig VanDerwater (2017).

Finding Mentor Authors

In this unit, instead of gathering a stack of published mentor texts, we look at what authors say about revision. While there are some published texts that show authors' revisions, most of the time you don't know what revision decisions an author made. Instead of texts, we will use video clips of what authors say about revision and their process for improving pieces of writing. To get started, go to www.authortoauthor.org.

     You will also need to collect examples of revisions in your own writing and student writing. At the end of any unit, it's helpful to save examples of interesting revision moves students have made. If you haven't been saving student samples, you can use the revisions students are making in their writing during the unit.

What Might I Teach?

Primary Goals

Students will make more intentional revision decisions.

or

Students will make independent revision decisions throughout the year. (You would have to wait until later in the year to truly be able to assess whether students have reached this goal.)

Possible Teaching Points

This unit has several possible groupings of minilessons. The groups of lessons you need will depend on the age of your students and their experience with revision.

Setting the Stage

Presumably, students have been revising already within other units of study, so the purpose of the immersion phase isn't to help students understand what revision is. Instead, spending the first day of this unit helping students understand the *importance* of revision will set the stage for what's to come. Your goal for this initial phase will be to understand what children are already thinking about revision, and perhaps help them reimagine what revision means. On this day you can use video clips of authors talking about revision, which can be found at www.authortoauthor.org.

You can also use actual examples of authors' revisions. I recently bought *Harry Potter: A History of Magic*, and not just for my Harry Potter fanatic daughter. Throughout the book, J. K. Rowling shows examples of her manuscripts and the handwritten revisions. A quick Google Images search for "J. K. Rowling revision" will show some of her revisions. In the author's note of the new edition of *The Mysterious Tadpole*, Steven Kellogg talks about revisions he made in this edition, twenty-five years after the original was published.

On these immersion days you might try the following:

* Ask students to share what they think revision means.

* Ask students to share their feelings about revision.

- Share your own examples of how looking at something more than once (revisiting, or re-visioning) helped you make it better. For example, every year I revise my teaching, I could share a change I made. Or I could say that I recently remodeled my kitchen and my final version was greatly revised from my original plan.

- Ask students to share examples of how trying something more than once helped them get better. For example, a child playing soccer is constantly revising their skills.

- Interview older students to talk about revision.

Mechanics of Revision

We want students to have access to every tool possible that allows them to revise without needing to recopy. What tools you choose depends on what your students need. Here are some tools you can offer and model as teaching points:

- Adding a page in between two pages
- Adding pages to your book
- Taking pages out of your book
- Adding a sentence by writing above
- Writing on the back
- Adding a word
- Crossing out a word or sentence
- Taping a slip of paper on to add a sentence
- Taping a half page to the side
- Adding a paragraph
- Using arrows to show where extra sentences go
- Using a number system to show where extra paragraphs go
- Knowing when to cross out and when to erase
- Using white tape to cover something up

Disposition Toward Revision

You might have several minilessons where the goal is to influence how children think about revision. Even though you started talking about this during the introduction day, that may not be enough. During the share/reflection time at the end of each writing workshop, you will share and celebrate revision decisions students made, which will further influence students' disposition toward revision. In addition to all of that, you might want these minilessons to focus on the benefits of revision:

- How to answer the question "What revision decisions have you made?"

- How to try out a revision, knowing you can always change it back to the way it was originally

Revision to Improve

Much of this unit will focus on how to improve the quality of writing through revision. Minilessons could include

- Looking at your writing through a lens of strengths

- Reflecting on your writing

- Setting goals for improving your writing

- Revising each day as you write

- Knowing when to add to your writing

- Changing word choice

- Changing sentence structure

- Knowing when to take something out; asking yourself, "Is it really needed?"

- Revising each day; rereading writing at the start of the day

- Making final revisions when you think you're almost done

Conferring

What to Carry with You

Since we don't have a stack of published mentor texts in this unit, our conferring kit will be limited to samples of student and teacher writing. Student writing will be particularly important if one of our goals is to improve students' disposition toward revision. Showing revision moves that other students have made, whether from previous years or your current class, reinforces the idea that revision is something their peers are doing and find beneficial.

In addition to student writing, you will need to carry samples of your own writing to show revisions you have made or are thinking you might make. When creating my own writing to teach with, I write at a level between published writing (so students can see my approximations) and student writing. However, that doesn't mean that I intentionally write poorly so I have something to revise. In any piece of my own writing, I can show authentic revision moves I might make.

What to Think About While Conferring

The first thing I look for is what revision decisions a student has made. I might be able to see some of those when looking at their writing in advance, but to really understand their thinking, I have to start by asking them. Most of my teaching in conferences is into revision.

In a conference with Kara (Video 12.2), she starts by explaining the introduction to her story and whether to keep a part in. I show her how I sometimes take something out of my writing, knowing that I can always put it back in. Kara decides to try this out. The goal in this conference is to teach a specific revision strategy.

In fourth-grader Mina's conference (Video 12.3) the focus isn't on a particular revision

Video 12.2

Kara's Conference

Video 12.3

Mina's Conference

strategy. Instead, the focus is on how to set goals for yourself as a writer. When I ask Mina what she's working on in this piece of writing, she isn't sure. I explain the revision skills I'm working on to show her what I mean, and then ask her whether she's working on adding things in, taking things out, changing parts of her writing, or moving parts of her writing. Mina decides on the more challenging goal of moving sections of her writing. The focus in this conference is to think about types of revisions that could help your writing and to set personal revision goals, rather than to teach a specific revision goal.

Both of these conferences are based on the assumption that writers revise their writing. Our expectation is that students will make revision decisions and try our various revision moves. I don't want to take ownership of their writing, and I will leave the decision of whether to keep the revision up to the student. This mindset is particularly helpful with children who are reluctant to revise. I can be more directive in asking them to *try* a particular revision move, but I leave the decision of whether to keep the revision in their writing up to them. Most of the time, students keep the revision in. We want all children to revise, not because we require it but because they have had positive revision experiences.

→ **For More on This Unit**

- *About the Authors: Writing Workshop with Our Youngest Writers* by Katie Wood Ray and Lisa B. Cleaveland

- *After the End: Teaching and Learning Creative Revision*, 2nd ed., by Barry Lane

- *Making Revision Matter: Strategies for Guiding Students to Focus, Organize, and Strengthen Their Writing Independently* by Janet Angelillo

- *Revision Decisions: Talking Through Sentences and Beyond* by Jeff Anderson and Deborah Dean

- *The Revision Toolbox: Teaching Techniques That Work*, 2nd ed., by Georgia Heard

- *Study Driven: A Framework for Planning Units of Study in the Writing Workshop* by Katie Wood Ray

- *Writing Workshop: The Essential Guide* by Ralph Fletcher and JoAnn Portalupi

Chapter 13

Genre Overview

or

What Types of Writing Do Writers Create?

or

Becoming More Intentional and Articulate About Genre

One of the benefits of craft and process studies is that they help students understand the concept of genre. What better way to engage students in learning specific characteristics of specific genres than to allow them to choose their own?

Second-grader Harrison has written in different genres throughout the year, but when I ask him in our conference what type of book he's going to make next, he isn't sure what to call it (Video 13.1). He knows the broad topic, Pokémon, and has narrowed it down to types of Pokémon. But he's not sure what to call the genre he's planning on writing in. He knows that his book is going to have facts, and knows a book that it's like (a Pokémon book at home), but he doesn't know how to describe or name this genre.

Harrison is typical of many second graders who aren't sure what genre they're writing in when they haven't been told what to make. Genre is a complex idea, and since Harrison can choose any genre, he needs to know how to think about the characteristics of whichever genre he chooses. He does show that he knows a bit about his genre by saying it's not a story. I help him figure out what it is by showing him two different published texts, *How to Heal a Broken Wing* by Bob Graham, a story, and *Frogs* by Gail Gibbons, an informational book. Harrison decides that his book will be more like *Frogs*. So I repeat my question from the beginning of the conference: "What type of book are you making?" Harrison replies with his own twist on the genre descriptor by saying, "A book that helps you learn facts about Pokémon." His description shows his understanding of genre better than if he had just said, "I'm making a nonfiction book."

Video 13.1

Harrison's Conference

Rationale for the Study

This unit helps students (and teachers) understand the idea of genre more deeply. Katie Wood Ray (2006) reminds us that genre isn't black and white—there's quite a lot of gray area, especially on the edges where one genre turns into another.

In workshops with teachers I sometimes give groups of teachers stacks of texts and ask them to divide them into two piles: texts that are organized as stories and texts that are organized as lists. Stories include characters, setting, plot, movement through time, and some type of change. Stories are texts about a time something happened. For example, *The Snowy Day* by Ezra Jack Keats is about the *time* Peter played in the snow. In the list pile, we put texts that are organized by sections, or facts or steps, or texts that are lists of thoughts about a topic. Think of your basic informational book or article. It's likely organized as a list of facts.

Sounds easy, right? It's actually not, especially when I deliberately add books that inhabit that gray area, and I often have teachers who get into heated story versus list debates, or who are adamant that they need a third pile. The point isn't to accurately identify whether a text is a story or a list. I've heard good cases on both sides for which pile *No, David!* by David Shannon goes in, and there is no court that will decree whether it is a story or a list. Our goal, instead, is to look at texts closely and understand how they work.

After this basic story/list sort, we then sort the texts by genre. What genre is *Snow* by Cynthia Rylant? What genre is *Bat Loves the Night* by Nicola Davies? There's often a fuzzy line between genres. Most informational writing has a stance, or sense of opinion, in it. And much of the opinion-based writing we read has information in it. It's not always easy to pinpoint where one genre ends and a related genre starts.

What's most important is the ability to build stacks of mentor texts that have similar characteristics. We want students to more deeply understand these genre characteristics so they can apply them in their own writing.

Beyond understanding genres, students should be able to realize the wide range of genres they might choose from. Some students have favorite genres they don't think they can write in school, while other students aren't even aware of genres outside those they've already studied in school.

⟶ **You might choose this study if . . .**

- *You want your students to understand genre more clearly throughout the rest of the year.*

- *Your students oversimplify the idea of genre ("It has photographs, so it must be an informational text.").*

- *You want to expand the range of genres students consider when choosing what to make.*

- *Your students often choose whichever genre they studied most recently or most frequently over the past few years.*

Grade Range

K–6. Students at any age should be articulate about their genre. Older students will have a much wider range of genres to consider and will be more likely to name a more specific genre, or a subgenre.

Time of Year

This unit could be placed at any point in the year when you want students to better understand the idea of genre. Often teachers and schools place this unit earlier in the year because it helps students consider and choose from a wide range of genres throughout the year. I know numerous teachers who launch the year with this study when their students already have a foundation of writing workshop routines and procedures from the previous year.

Student Learning and the Writing Celebration

When sharing in partnerships, in small groups, or with the whole class, students can explain which genre they chose and why. Older students might talk about why they chose the particular genre as well as their topic and audience. Instead of just naming and describing their genre, they could name examples of published texts in the same genre.

Students might also share what genre they plan on writing the next time they have the opportunity to choose their genre. We want students always thinking forward about what they will make next, which strengthens their identity as a writer.

Key Unit Questions

What are you making?
    or
What type of writing are you creating?
    or
What genre are you writing in?

These questions are at the very heart of this book. If I had to come up with a key question that could be asked at the beginning of every unit in this book, one of these would be it. They can be asked only in craft and process studies—studies in which students are able to choose their own genre.

Gathering Published Mentor Texts

You will need to collect a large stack of texts in this unit because you will need access to a wide range of genres. If this isn't your first unit of the year, you could pull texts students already know as readers, which will offer a little extra support as they start thinking more deeply about genre. If you are using unfamiliar texts, shorter pieces are best.

You might pull some texts that fall into the gray area of genre so students can engage in a debate about what genre they are. You might choose texts on the same topic but from different genres. You might also have on hand some genres that your students might not think of choosing, like graphic short stories, video game reviews, or how-to writing.

You will also need student samples to show that students have tried out various genres. It's helpful for students to see approximations of genres, especially genres they think might be harder to try out.

What Might I Teach?

Primary Goals

Students will make more intentional genre decisions.

or

Students will understand genre more deeply.

or

Students will explain the genre they are writing in and what makes it that genre.

Possible Teaching Points

Immersion

I often start this unit by asking students to think about what types of books or texts go together in a stack. I then pull two books on the same topic in different genres. These are easy to find. I might pull

- *Frogs* (list) by Gail Gibbons and one of the Frog and Toad books (story) by Arnold Lobel or one of the Froggy books (story) by Jonathan London;

- *Roller Coaster* (story) by Marla Frazee and an informational book about roller coasters (list);

- *Long Shot* by Chris Paul (story) and *Chris Paul* (list) by Jeff Savage from the Amazing Athletes series.

We read the two books and talk about how they are similar and different. We then examine other books we have read, talk about them, and decide which of the original two books they are more like. I intentionally choose books that make this trickier and will cause some debate. I might pull a story book that has photographs, since students sometimes think photographs equal informational books. Students in some grades will go right for the fiction-nonfiction distinction, which in writing can be confusing. For example, where do the true stories go? True stories (or personal narratives) aren't fictional, make-believe stories, and they also aren't informational books that teach facts about a person.

If the debate isn't as lively as I'd hope, I might pull in a book like *Bat Loves the Night*, which has both a story layer of text and an informational layer of text. When a book includes two types of texts, which wins out? When students notice this book's index, they might swing toward naming it an informational book, but when they think about the main character, they might swing back toward story.

The best-case scenario for these first couple of days of immersion is that students' debates deepen and become more heated. I'm in no hurry to clarify their confusions. The struggle helps them better understand genre in the long run.

With older students, you might choose complex texts. Since they may know more about genre, you might spend more time having them categorize stacks of texts on their own. You might put out all sorts of texts from a range of genres and encourage children to come up with their own categories. It's easier to do this with texts they already know, and if you're using texts they don't know, the texts will need to be fairly short. Picture books work well for this, even in the upper grades.

Introducing or Exploring Various Genres

The bulk of this unit will be spent exploring specific genres. We're not trying to become experts in any genre by studying it for a day or two. Instead, we're just trying to understand it well enough so that we can describe it clearly.

In the primary grades, we use picture books to explore genres. We might spend a day or two exploring these texts:

- true stories that happened to the author
- realistic fiction
- fiction
- fairy tales
- informational all-about books
- how-to books
- poetry
- reviews
- any other genres students might encounter and want to try out

In the upper grades, we go beyond picture books. For example, we might use realistic fiction short stories from children's magazines rather than realistic fiction picture books. We could also study a broader range of genres. In the upper grades we might study the following genres:

- true stories
- memoirs

- short realistic fiction

- short fiction stories

- mysteries

- fantasy

- feature articles

- reviews

- graphic short stories

- how-to articles

- essays and commentaries

- poetry and songs

- any other genres students might encounter and try out

The aim is not simply to expose students to as many genres as possible, but rather to provide a wide enough range of genres that they start to notice differences and similarities between genres.

Choosing Genres

In addition to helping students understand a variety of genres, we might support students in choosing genres. We encourage students to have and choose favorite genres, but it's helpful as well to encourage them to consider new or different genres. We might have lessons on

- Trying out a genre you haven't written in before

- How to match your topic with various genres

- How to write on the same topic in a different genre

Conferring

What to Carry with You

During this unit my conferring kit might be a little bigger, simply because I might carry more genres with me. With young students who are working to figure out what genre they are writing in, I might have two books with me and ask the child which book their writing is more like. For example, when a young child is trying to figure out if they are writing a story or a book that tells a lot about something, I might show them a story they know and an informational book they know and ask them which type of book they are making.

What to Think About While Conferring

I am more interested in students' understanding of genre and the characteristics of genres than in their ability to identify their genre. I'm more interested in a child's ability to say, "I'm writing one of those make-believe books that could really happen" than a child's ability to say, "I'm writing realistic fiction" when the child can't describe what that means. So, at the beginning of conferences in this unit, I am likely to ask students to tell me what genre they are writing in. With older students I ask how their genre fits with their topic, purpose, and audience.

When I ask Deetya in our conference what type of book she's making, she replies the way many first graders do (Video 13.2). She tells me the topic—"It's a nature book"—rather than the genre. I decide to show her how authors think about genre before they start and show her three different genres: a story book, an informational book, and a list book (the particular book I show her, *Mud* by Mary Lyn Ray, could be called an ode or illustrated poetry). It's important to give her actual examples. (If I were Deetya's teacher, I would pull out only books she already knows.)

I model with my own writing, showing her that I'm thinking about writing about playing basketball with my son and need to decide which genre to write in. It could be a story about the first time my son beat me playing basketball, or a book that's all about how wonderful basketball is, or a book that teaches people about basketball.

When I ask her to try this, she tells me that her nature book is really an informational book. But, when I ask her what type of book she's going to make next, she goes right back to topic and says, "My birthday." This isn't surprising and shows that understanding genre develops over time. I ask her which one of the three books on her desk her birthday book will be like, and she quickly decides it will be a true story.

Video 13.2

Deetya's Conference

In a conference, you might also ask students *why* they chose a particular genre. In Chapter 1, in Video 1.2: Fifth Graders Talk About Genre Choices, this question elicited a wide range of reasons. You might also ask students what other genres they might write in during the unit. The goal is not to encourage or discourage particular genres, or to limit or steer their choices, but to inspire them to actively consider and choose from a wide range of genres, rather than reverting back to whatever genre they have written most frequently or recently.

⟶ For More on This Unit

- *About the Authors: Writing Workshop with Our Youngest Writers* by Katie Wood Ray and Lisa B. Cleaveland

- *Study Driven: A Framework for Planning Units of Study in the Writing Workshop* by Katie Wood Ray

Chapter 14

Illustration Study

or

Composing with Pictures and Words

or

Thinking in Greater Detail in Pictures in Words

or

Using Illustrations and Text to Support Each Other

Early in the school year, first-grade teacher Megan Ralstron wanted her children to think, speak, and write in greater detail. To support their compositional thinking in writing, Megan decided to focus a unit on how children could use illustrations to improve the quality of their writing. In this illustration study, Megan and the students noticed a wide range of techniques that published illustrators used and tried these techniques out in their own books.

On the day I taught Megan's classroom, we studied the technique of using more than one illustration on a page. Illustrators use this technique in different genres, for a variety of reasons. An informational book illustrator might use two pictures to show a bullfrog's air sac before and after it croaks, while a story illustrator might show a series of small actions like Gaia Cornwall does in *Jabari Jumps*, the book I use in the minilesson in Video 14.1. After we talk about some of the techniques students already noticed and tried out, I show them how Gaia uses this technique to show how Jabari climbs to the top of the diving board. Using more than one picture on a page is a relatively simple thing for students to try, but I want to make sure it actually affects their writing. So I also show them how Gaia uses more than one sentence for each picture. I want them to clearly see how she uses both her pictures and her words to help readers understand this key moment in the book.

I model with my own writing and end by encouraging them to think about how they might try out this technique in their books. One student sums up the point of this technique well when he says, "It tells the people more about your book." Thinking about your reader and how to help them understand is important for students in any grade, in any genre—an illustration study can be a great way in to this work.

Rationale for the Study

This unit supports compositional thinking by helping children become more intentional and thoughtful about using illustrations to enhance meaning in their writing. In her seminal book

Video 14.1

Minilesson: More Than One
Illustration on a Page

In Pictures and In Words (2010), Katie Wood Ray lays out several compelling reasons for illustration study, including complete chapters on each of these ideas:

- building stamina

- writing and illustrating as parallel processes

- teaching an essential habit of mind: reading like writers

- learning qualities of good writing from illustration techniques

Each chapter lays another brick in the foundation of this fundamental idea: that we can support children's compositional thinking in words by supporting the compositional thinking in their pictures.

It's also important to remember that the goal of this unit isn't beautiful illustrations (although students will certainly create interesting illustrations). Instead, the goal is for detailed illustrations *to make an impact on their writing*. More detailed illustrations support more detailed oral language—which in turn leads to more detailed writing.

→ **You might choose this study if . . .**

- *You teach kindergarten, since illustrations are crucial in communicating meaning for young writers.*

- *You teach first or second grade and you want to increase the compositional thinking of your students.*

- *You teach upper grades and want a different way of helping your students understand the qualities of good writing.*

- *Your students see illustrations as decoration that comes after the fact, rather than as an important compositional tool.*

- *You want to increase the compositional thinking of students in genre studies throughout the year.*

Grade Range

K–2. This study appears more typically in the primary grades, although it can certainly make an impact in upper grades as well. You'll notice that the next chapter describes a picture book unit specifically for intermediate grades—that unit has a different focus. In the primary grades, our stack of mentor texts is almost always picture books, so almost *every* unit is a picture book study. The stack of picture books is organized around various ideas (genre, process, or craft). In the intermediate grades, teachers might choose to study picture books almost as a genre unto itself, to pay attention to how graphics and picture books work together to convey meaning. That type of intermediate-grade picture book study is described in Chapter 15.

Time of Year

This study would typically come early in the year in kindergarten since students are relying on illustrations to carry much of the meaning in their books. In first and second grade it would also make sense early in the year, but it could be placed at any point in the year.

Student Learning and the Writing Celebration

The goal of the unit is for students' illustrations and text to work together to create meaning. Therefore, during the celebration, in addition to celebrating their writing, students could

- show a specific place in their writing where their pictures and words support each other;

- highlight their most interesting illustration technique;

- show an illustration technique they tried out and the page in the mentor text where they learned the technique;

- show a place in their writing where they took a risk to try out a challenging technique, thereby celebrating the risk taking more than the skill.

During the celebration we will marvel at the changes in their composing and thinking since the beginning of the unit.

Key Unit Questions

What is the most interesting illustration technique you have tried out?
    or
Where do your illustrations and text support each other?

Gathering Published Mentor Texts

There are a couple of things to think about in an illustration study. As in other craft studies, you'll want to make sure that a variety of genres are represented. You'll also want to include several books that include multiple techniques. Based on the books on the shelves next to me right now (or, more accurately, in piles on the floor throughout my office), here's a possible stack and the thinking behind each book:

- *How to Heal a Broken Wing* by Bob Graham: A realistic fiction book that has numerous techniques; a book I love and one that students would already know from me reading it earlier in the year.

- *Frogs* by Gail Gibbons: An informational book with a variety of techniques, including some less common techniques that are good for informational text.

- *Walk On!* by Marla Frazee: A how-to book with a variety of techniques.

- *Dylan's Day Out* by Peter Catalanotto: A fiction book packed with different techniques on each page.

- *Red Sled* by Lita Judge: A fiction book with a large variety of techniques.

- A Pigeon book or one of the Elephant and Piggie books by Mo Willems: A fiction book that is great for facial expressions and body posture.

- *Tough Boris* by Mem Fox: A book in which the text has more of a list structure but a story is told in the illustrations; a variety of techniques are used.

- *Zombie in Love* by Kelly DiPucchio: A fiction book with an engaging topic.

- *Amazing Powers* by Catherine Saunders: An informational superhero book with interesting techniques; it could also be used in an informational unit later in the year.

This is simply one example of a stack that represents a variety of genres—it includes some texts that have lots of techniques in one book, and a few books that are good examples of specific techniques. You will, of course, choose your own stack to reflect your needs and your teaching goals.

What Might I Teach?

Primary Goals

Students will use a variety of illustration techniques to enhance meaning.
>   or
Students will intentionally use techniques to write and illustrate in greater detail.

Possible Teaching Points

Immersion

Often I start this unit by modeling what I mean by noticing illustration techniques. I'll read the first story of *Dog and Bear: Two Friends, Three Stories* by Laura Vaccaro Seeger. I use this story because it's really short and uses a variety of techniques in its ten or so pages. After I point out a few techniques I notice, students will begin to notice other techniques. Partners then go off with sticky notes and a book that has interesting techniques to see what they notice. Partnerships will then share out what they have noticed, and we'll start our anchor chart of techniques. As in many craft and process studies, you don't have to have an immersion phase. But my experience has been that students' illustrations will look very different right away after just two immersion days.

> Having an immersion phase or a setting-the-stage lesson in a craft or process unit accelerates learning and supports students in working toward unit goals right from the start.

Taking Risks

You might need a couple of minilessons to help students take risks and draw things they don't know how to draw. I generally teach these techniques:

- Think about what color you need.

- Think about what shapes you see, or what's the biggest shape.

- Think about the parts you need.

- Don't switch to something else—draw it the best you can.

You might also need a minilesson on how to respond to classmates' illustrations in ways that make them feel comfortable taking risks to draw things that are hard to draw.

Understanding Illustration Techniques

I can't urge you strongly enough to read *In Pictures and In Words* (Ray 2010), where fifty different illustration techniques are paired with corresponding writing techniques. There's no need for me to list all of them here. Instead, here are a few of the techniques that student are likely to try out in the primary grades:

- Drawing people in different ways (front, side, in motion, hairstyles, etc.)

- Including background details—location (inside or outside), time of day, season, and so on

- Showing emotions through facial expressions and body posture

- Zooming in/out in an illustration

- Showing movement through a variety of techniques

- Using multiple illustrations on the page

- Creating illustrations that go off the page

As in most units, you could spend multiple days on any technique.

Supporting the Connection Between Pictures and Words

You may want to include some lessons that focus on ensuring that the level of composition in the text is increasing along with the level of composition in the illustrations. Lessons could include

- Elaborating in your writing based on what you included in the illustration

- Reflecting on whether your pictures and words support each other

- Determining whether the level of detail in your illustration and the level of detail in your words are equivalent

Process

- Illustrating with color rather than coloring in

- Adding to pictures

- Changing a picture without starting over

Conferring

What to Carry with You

The conferring kit is fairly straightforward for this unit. I include a couple of favorite texts from my stack and a writing sample where I've tried out several techniques. (Remember, you would have this anyway since you would have to try out some techniques before you taught them to students.) Finally, you will need a couple of examples of student writing where students have tried out various techniques.

What to Think About While Conferring

Whether we are looking at student writing at the beginning of a conference or for a few minutes before the start of the school day, we will want to look for the level of detail in illustrations and the level of composition in their words (or oral language with very young writers). You will also want to look for evidence that students are trying out new techniques and taking risks in their illustrations.

Just as you will want to have various genres represented in your stack, ideally you will have student and teacher samples from more than one genre.

In first-grader Jude's conference (Video 14.2), I decide to show him how he can zoom in or out in an illustration. Students often draw each page the same way. When they draw a page that looks different from the others, we have an insight into their thinking. I want Jude to know that authors use this technique in different genres, so I first show him how Bob Graham does it in *How to Heal a Broken Wing* and then how Gail Gibbons does it in *Frogs*.

I also show him how a student tried it out, and at this point he makes a connection. Jude shows me that he's already like those authors by getting a different book of his out of his folder and showing me a page where he already zoomed in (Figure 14.1). But he hadn't thought about trying it in his current book. By connecting what he did to what mentor illustrators do, I am strengthening his identity as a writer and an illustrator.

Allie is a kindergartner and her book shows an incredible number of illustration techniques—motion lines, multiple illustrations on a page, depiction of feelings through facial expressions and body posture, and many more (Figure 14.2). What's more impressive is how purposeful her illustration decisions are. To build on these amazing illustrations, in Allie's conference (Video 14.3) I show her how she could write a bit more about what she's showing in each illustration. The language she composes for the illustration, "I was feeling so happy I cried," expertly supports the meaning she is conveying in her illustration.

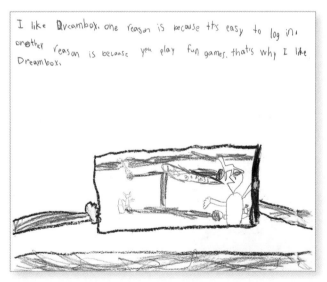

Figure 14.1 Jude's Zoomed-In Illustration

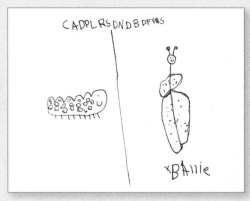

Figure 14.2 Allie's Book

Video 14.2

Jude's Conference

Video 14.3

Allie's Conference

⟶ **For More on This Unit**

- *In Pictures and In Words: Teaching the Qualities of Good Writing Through Illustration Study* by Katie Wood Ray

- *Talking, Drawing, Writing: Lessons for Our Youngest Writers* by Martha Horn and Mary Ellen Giacobbe

Chapter 15

Using Illustrations and Text to Create Meaning in the Upper Grades

or

Making Picture Books in the Upper Grades

Much of this unit is based on the work of and conversations with Katherine Bomer.

Eden, a fourth grader, has chosen to write a fairly complex realistic fiction story about a girl who runs away from home. Eden has stapled paper together into a book and has started to include a few illustrations. She's thinking of this as a chapter book with a few illustrations. I'm thinking that she could write this as a picture book by thinking slightly more about how her pictures and text work together. It won't alter the amount of text and illustrations, but will shift her thinking since the illustrations in a picture book matter.

There are numerous picture books that tackle serious topics, contain sophisticated text, and are appropriate for intermediate-grade students. One side goal of my conference with Eden (Video 15.1) is to help her think of picture books as worthy of study. My teaching point is to think ahead about how to have your illustrations and text work together, rather than adding illustrations as decoration or an afterthought when you're finished.

I show Eden how I am thinking about my illustrations while I write by using a storyboard kind of sketch right in my text. I put a couple of small sketches in the margin of my own story. I also show her how to plan with a storyboard. The storyboard is composed of illustrations of the key events in the story. In addition to using it to plan, students can also use it to think ahead about their illustrations. Eden decides to include sketches as she goes, which won't take her much time. But the thinking she's engaging in to compose her illustrations mirrors the composing she's doing with her words—which is what we hope for in a study like this one.

Video 15.1
Eden's Conference

Rationale for the Study

In this unit older students will study how pictures and words in a picture book create meaning, regardless of the genre. There is some overlap between this unit and the illustration study described in the previous chapter. In both studies, we consider how pictures and text support each other to make meaning. In the primary grades, however, picture books are usually the default since that's what students are more familiar with. Meaning, learning is maximized when students envision and create from models they know best. In this unit, we're studying picture books as a thing to make. Often in the intermediate grades, we don't tend to think about graphics or how they work with text. (In the primary grades, you can't help but study this unless you purposefully devalue illustrations.) So the very idea of making a picture book might be new to intermediate-grade teachers and students, and therefore worthy of study.

When we make picture books, we aren't making simple books written for very young children. Instead, our stack of mentor texts is composed of very sophisticated picture books, and students will be making books with an audience of peers and adults in mind.

Throughout the year, students might be engaging in other types of writing for which graphics are important. Most informational writing, whether feature articles, how-to articles, list articles, biographical sketches, or some other genre, relies on graphics to convey meaning and support text. Some opinion writing, such as video game reviews, public service announcements, and Ted Talks, also uses graphics to make or clarify a point. Students might study graphic short stories or historical fiction picture books as types of narrative writing. Considering how graphics and text work together in a picture book study will influence their writing in other units as well.

We also want students to understand crafting techniques in writing. Katie Wood Ray (2010) makes the case that authors and illustrators use the same techniques to engage a reader. Students can actually see the technique in an illustration, and for some learners seeing a technique will make it more concrete. By showing the same craft move in both illustrations and text, we can help students better understand how to use that technique to affect a reader.

⟶ You might choose this study if . . .

- *You want to enhance the compositional thinking and language of your intermediate-grade students.*

- *You want students to be more thoughtful about how text and graphics work together in genre studies throughout the year.*

- *You want to engage students, especially students for whom art and illustration is a powerful entry into writing.*

Grade Range

3–6. In grades 3–6, students aren't typically making picture books. In this unit students have the opportunity to study picture books as a type of writing, but of course they could choose to write in any genre of picture books.

Time of Year

This study could be placed at any point in the year. Placing it early in the year can strengthen students' compositional thinking, which will benefit them throughout the year. Placing it in the middle or later part of the year might increase engagement in writing at a time when energy for writing might normally lag.

Student Learning and the Writing Celebration

This unit lends itself well to a celebration where students have an opportunity to both see and hear classmates' books by doing a combination of a gallery walk and reading their writing in small groups. During the gallery walk, students read each other's books and leave sticky note compliments for the author/illustrator. Each student might have a published mentor text open next to their book to show an inspiration for a portion of their own book.

Since the focus is on the text as well as the illustrations, it's great if students have a chance to read their books aloud. During the gallery walk students might be more inclined to comment on the illustrations, so reading their books aloud helps reinforce the focus on both pictures and words.

This is a unit where I might actually be cautious about having a celebration with a kindergarten or first-grade buddy class. In the upper grades we often tell students early on in the unit whom they will be sharing their writing with during the celebration at the end of the unit, to help them have an audience in mind. If we tell them they will be sharing with five-year-olds, they will be more likely to make less complex books. If you do decide to share with much younger children, explain to your students that you're sharing to give the younger children a vision for what they will do someday—and reinforce that writers at any age think about pictures and words.

Key Unit Question

How do your pictures and text support each other?

Since this is a writing unit, this question will help reinforce for students that our goal is for them to think in greater detail and compose with more intention.

Gathering Published Mentor Texts

You will, of course, want to choose books that are engaging and meaningful to your students. Older students are able to handle much more complex and serious topics, and there are many picture books that use text and illustrations to tackle significant issues.

You will also want to include books in which the illustrations convey and enhance meaning—if you didn't have the illustrations, you wouldn't fully understand the book, or if the illustrations were different, the meaning would change.

You want picture books where the illustrations matter and aren't just there as decorations. Interestingly, in some books that have less text, the illustrations do more of the work, so you might actually want some books that have a bit less text. *Baseball Saved Us* by Ken Mochizuki, for example, is a picture book about a boy playing baseball in a Japanese internment camp. The illustrations and color choice affect the overall tone of the book, and techniques like placing a series of illustrations on the same page help create tension. These techniques are reflected in the text, and the text and illustrations work together to engage the reader differently than text alone would. It's particularly important to include a variety of genres in this stack—we tend to have the impulse to choose primarily stories when picking books with beautiful illustrations, rather than also including some books that are organized as a list that also have beautiful illustrations and language.

What Might I Teach?

Primary Goal

Students will create picture books in which the illustration techniques and craft techniques work together to convey powerful messages.

Possible Teaching Points

Immersion

During the first several days of this unit, students will spend time noticing how illustrations and text work together to create meaning. The books that you share with students at this stage will quickly communicate what types of books they will be creating. Choose books with interesting, sophisticated language rather than books with simple language written for much younger students. Choose examples where the illustrations affect tone and meaning.

Understanding Illustration Techniques

The key to this unit is that students are studying and making picture books. This isn't a unit where we show a literary technique in a picture book and then try it out in a short story. Therefore, students and teachers will need to understand techniques illustrators *and* authors use.

The best place to go to understand illustration techniques is Katie Wood Ray's book *In Pictures and In Words* (2010). Katie names fifty illustration techniques and shows examples in which authors use the same techniques in writing, often in texts other than picture books. Here are just a few of the many techniques students might notice and try out:

- Creating illustrations that affect the mood and tone
- Using illustrations to convey additional meaning
- Placing illustrations and text strategically on the page
- Showing more in the illustration than in the words
- Creating illustrations that amplify and emphasize the text
- Crafting tone with color
- Revealing character traits by adding background details to illustrations
- Showing passage of time through illustrations
- Manipulating point of view through illustrations
- Using perspective

Process

- Honoring approximations and taking risks in illustrations
- Thinking about illustrations from the start
- Planning by using a storyboard or mock book
- Composing text
- Revising text and illustrations
- Using page turns for effect
- Considering and writing for a specific audience

Conferring

What to Carry with You

In this unit you will rely heavily on both your own writing and your stack of published texts. Depending on your students' recent experience with using illustrations and text to support each other, you may need to do a fair amount of envisioning for students to be able to see what they might try in their own books. Some students will be able to try out a technique just by seeing it in published mentor texts, but many will need to see what it looks like when you try it out yourself.

Some (or many) students may not be comfortable with their perceived illustration skills and abilities. They may feel they don't illustrate particularly well. It's important that when we use our own writing, we show and celebrate how approximate our own illustrations are. If you are a skilled illustrator, you will actually need to illustrate less well in front of your students. Your students already have a vision of what professional illustrators do. Instead, they need to see your approximations.

The range of student confidence levels is also why we need to teach with student samples. Children need to see examples of children trying out illustration and writing techniques in very approximate ways. When you are saving samples at the end of the unit to use the following year, be sure to save a range of skill levels rather than just saving your five most beautifully illustrated books. Also, you probably have some students who are much more skilled and confident in illustrating than they are in writing. Using their books to teach with provides an opportunity to lift up their status as a composer in the class.

What to Think About While Conferring

Because the goal is for children to compose with both pictures and words, it's helpful to ask how they are using their text and illustrations to support each other. The thinking behind what they're attempting with their illustration is more interesting than the actual execution of an illustration technique. Once we hear what a child is thinking, we can support them in trying it out, doing it better, or trying out other options.

In conferences it is important to balance out the emphasis on text and illustrations to make sure students are focusing on both. Some less confident illustrators might naturally focus more on text and take fewer risks in illustrations, and the more confident illustrators might spend little time on the text. We want to make sure we nudge students to develop their skills in both areas.

In Eden's conference (Video 15.1), I use myself as the mentor as I show her how I think about illustrations as I write. I don't often write or draw in front of students during a conference, or in a minilesson for that matter. If students are just watching me draw or write, they're not learning anything. Usually I write or draw ahead of time and show students what I did, or I compose in the air and actually draw or write later. In this case, I want Eden to see how quick and easy it is to do, so I draw in the moment.

I also want this conference to be fairly invitational, so I give her a couple of options on what to do next. Eden appears to be agreeable and interested in adding storyboard illustrations, so I don't feel the need to be more directive. With another student, I might be more directive about having the student try it out to get a feel for it.

→ For More on this Unit

- *In Pictures and In Words: Teaching the Qualities of Good Writing Through Illustration Study* by Katie Wood Ray

- *In the Company of Children* by Joanne Hindley

Chapter 16

How to Make Paragraphing Decisions

or

Using Paragraphs to Craft Text and Make Writing Easy to Read

Learning how to make paragraphing decisions isn't necessarily at the top of the list of the most engaging units of study for students. But it's much more engaging if students have personally meaningful genres and topics. When students care more about their writing, there is an increased desire for it to be easily understood by their reader.

Anisha identifies paragraphing as a need right at the beginning of her conference (Video 16.1). She explains how she is currently thinking about paragraphs and identifies a specific place where she's wondering whether she needs a new paragraph. This shows a lot about what she already knows about paragraphing.

I show Anisha how two mentors are trying out a change to their writing to see how it feels. I show how Kara is thinking about taking sentences out, and how I'm thinking about a paragraph decision of my own. By having Anisha read her writing aloud and try out the new paragraph, I extend the teaching beyond this teaching point to the broader idea of trying out a change in your writing to see how it feels.

Rationale for the Study

In this unit students will think more deeply about the decisions authors make about paragraphs. Students and teachers sometimes think that writing a single paragraph is a skill students need. However, until you have enough writing on a page to require more than one paragraph, there is little benefit in thinking about paragraphs. The purpose of paragraphs is to make writing easier to read, whether it's by breaking up long sections of text by indenting or by grouping ideas into chunks of text. Therefore, in this unit the focus will be on how to make paragraphing decisions within a longer piece rather than on how to write a single, isolated paragraph. If students need to write a single paragraph for an assessment, then you can prepare them for that experience in the same way you might handle other test-related skills, such as writing to a prompt—you could have a mini-unit on writing for an assessment, or you could practice the skill in small doses throughout the year.

It's important that students understand that there are not rigid rules that govern paragraphs. The more rigid students think the rules are, the fewer decisions they have to make. All authors

Video 16.1
Anisha's Conference

have options and are constantly making their own decisions—including decisions about paragraphs. By helping students to understand the purposes of paragraphs, we help them understand the impact paragraphing decisions have on readers.

→ **You might choose this study if . . .**

- *You want to accelerate your students' understanding of paragraphs and paragraphing decisions in all genres.*

- *Your students are not currently using paragraphs or think that paragraphs have rigid rules.*

- *You want to add energy to a topic that students often see as less engaging.*

Grade Range

3–6. This unit is saved for the intermediate grades, at which point students are writing enough text to organize into paragraphs. When younger children are making picture books, the page turn often does the same work as indenting a paragraph. Younger students might have more than one paragraph on a page in a picture book and will need to learn about paragraphs for other types of writing, such as reviews. But this unit will have more of an impact when most of the writing children are producing has multiple paragraphs.

Time of Year

This unit could be placed at any point in the year. Like many studies, placing it early in the year will allow students to benefit from their increased skill throughout the year. In third grade I would want to make sure students were at a point in their writing where they needed paragraphs, so it might not be the first unit of the year.

Student Learning and the Writing Celebration

For this celebration students will show what they've learned about paragraphing by highlighting some of their paragraphing decisions. For some students simply having paragraphs will represent new learning, while other students might explain their most interesting paragraphing decisions. Students could show a place where they thought about making a different paragraphing decision but decided not to. This would help put the focus on the thinking rather than the product, since the thinking is what will affect future pieces of writing. And, of course, we don't want the focus on paragraphing to take away from the sharing of pieces of writing students care about, so we will want to make sharing paragraph decisions just one aspect of the celebration.

Key Unit Questions

Where is a place in your writing where you aren't sure about a paragraph decision?
    or
How is it going with your paragraphing decisions?

    Both of these questions underscore the idea that authors make decisions about paragraphs.

Gathering Published Mentor Texts

Since you need to have more than one paragraph to make decisions about paragraphs (there's no decision to make if you only have one), stacks for this unit will include complete texts—short stories, articles, essays, reviews, or anything that is organized into paragraphs. I would tend not to include picture books unless I wanted to look at how a page turn works in a similar way to a paragraph. The key is to make sure that a variety of genres are represented in your stack. It's definitely important to include some stories since paragraphing in stories works differently, especially with dialogue. But you will also need to include genres other than stories. You might also pull from stacks from other units students have had, or will have, during the year. My stack in this unit might include

- a fiction or fantasy short story;

- a short story that happened to someone;

- a feature article;

- a how-to article;

- a review or essay.

Some genres lend themselves less well to this study. Graphic short stories (easy to find in children's magazines and highly engaging for students) aren't typically organized into multiple paragraphs. While poetry certainly requires students to make decisions on how to organize text, generally poetry doesn't include paragraphs. I would recommend not including these genres if

- there are other craft and process studies in your year where students will have unlimited choice of genre, or

- there are graphic short stories and/or poetry studies at another point in your year, or in the year before or after.

    In deciding on whether to include any unit, it's important to keep in mind the other units students are experiencing and to think about what opportunities students have to write in genres of choice throughout the year.

What Might I Teach?

Primary Goal

Students will make more intentional paragraphing decisions in this unit and throughout the rest of the year.

Possible Teaching Points

Immersion

In this unit we will start by studying a stack of texts representing a range of genres that utilize paragraphs. We might pull pieces of writing from other units in the year, but we will also open up genre possibilities by selecting some genres students may not have studied previously. The goal is to help students learn to notice paragraph decisions and to categorize the types of decisions authors make.

Crafting with Paragraphs

- What paragraphs do
- One-sentence paragraphs
- One-word paragraphs
- Intentionally long paragraphs

Paragraphing in Stories

- Paragraphing when writing dialogue
- Starting a new paragraph when there is a change in action
- Starting a new paragraph when there is a change in setting (or location or time)
- Starting a new paragraph when someone new is talking

Paragraphing in Expository Writing

- Paragraphing in informational text
- Paragraphing in how-to articles or procedural writing
- Paragraphing in essays and reviews

- Working with one-paragraph sections

- Using more than one paragraph in a section

Conferring

What to Carry with You

In addition to your stack of published mentor texts, you will also need samples of your own writing where you have made paragraphing decisions. It's helpful to have your own writing in several genres on hand, so you might pull samples from other units. You might also start a new piece of writing in a genre you haven't had a unit about.

In any craft or process study, you might need minilessons on choosing genres and choosing topics. If your students are choosing a narrow range of genres, a minilesson or two on choosing genres and picking a genre to go with a specific topic will help ensure students are choosing a genre rather than reverting back to what they have written most recently.

Student writing samples can be particularly powerful in this unit. Students encounter paragraphs constantly when they are reading, but the process published authors use to get there is invisible. Showing how other students in the class are using paragraphs can make paragraphing feel more achievable and meaningful to students.

What to Think About While Conferring

Looking at student writing in advance makes conferring more efficient. In this unit, when you are studying student writing, the first things you will want to pay attention to are whether the student is using paragraphs and whether their paragraphing decisions make sense. At the start of a conference, ask the child to talk about their paragraphing decisions. Depending on what they say and what they already know about paragraphing, you might teach them how to make better paragraphing decisions. As with any unit, if their paragraphing decisions are solid, you could then teach a writing skill or technique that is not related to paragraphing but cuts across any genre. Or, even if the child needs support in paragraphing, there may be another skill they need more. Teaching the child something about making paragraphing decisions (unit goal) or other skills and techniques (across genres) will be more beneficial than teaching something very specific to the genre they are writing in.

→ For More on This Unit

- *Study Driven: A Framework for Planning Units of Study in the Writing Workshop* by Katie Wood Ray

Chapter 17

General
Craft Study

or

Techniques Writers Use
to Make Their Writing
Interesting

Justin and his classmates in Sonya Weber's fifth grade are in a year-long rap battle with a teaching assistant, Mr. Tennyson. During the morning meeting in Justin's class, students can sign up to share any topic they feel comfortable sharing. Early in the year, Mr. Tennyson signed up to share and proceeded to do a rap that included the names of every student in the class. The rap centered on a fictitious disagreement between Sonya and him, and urged the students to join his side.

Sonya said, "This fired the students up! They laughed at his witty rhymes and oohed and aahed at his clever word choice as he provided 'burns' and 'digs' at the students. And because his rap put him in the position of Mr. Tennyson versus The Class, students immediately wanted revenge! The students came together and showed great camaraderie, which was *exactly* what was needed for the start of a new school year."

Students began responding during morning meeting with raps of their own, aimed at Mr. Tennyson. The raps had to be written and rehearsed. As of February of the school year (when I'm writing this), students have written and performed forty-three raps, with more to come. The raps are being collected in a binder and will be typed up and shared at the end of the year. It's an amazing example of engaged students writing independently for authentic purposes.

On the day I sit down next to Justin for his conference (Video 17.1), I am tempted to dig into his memoir about his sister going to college (Figure 17.1). But he seems to have more energy for talking about the rap he wrote (Figure 17.2), and I can't pass up the opportunity to talk about (and teach into) a genre I know little about.

Since Justin feels comfortable rapping out loud, I can hear how his rap sounds. I decide to rely on my limited rap knowledge and teach him how Lin-Manuel Miranda sometimes breaks his rhyme scheme on purpose (Miranda and McCarter 2016,

That Someone
By Justin

Have you ever missed somebody you loved, but didn't like at times when they were being mean? That someone is my sister, her name is cece and just went to college. This was when I was age 9 or 8.

I was relieved, happy. Then it hit me: I was alone with nobody to play with. I knew she could not just magically appear when I wanted her to.

For the first time I had the tv or myself. I couldn't stop thinking about my sister just saying "Let me get on the tv!" I was sad.

All those times she had made me mad. My sister was somebody who would be nice or mean. I had to learn to beat this pain. Some way, somehow, I had to!

I actually got a new phone, and we kept in contact. I realized she was being mean because of 'tough love', but also just love. My sister had helped me with some important and hard things, like my mom's divorce with my dad. My sister makes me happy most of the time, but like I've said, she also makes me mad sometimes. ut my sister is my sister and the important thing is love I love my sister. I understand now what my sister was doing, which is showing me the real world or giving me a taste of what some people will do to you, in the end, I thank my sister for everything.

Figure 17.1 Justin's Memoir

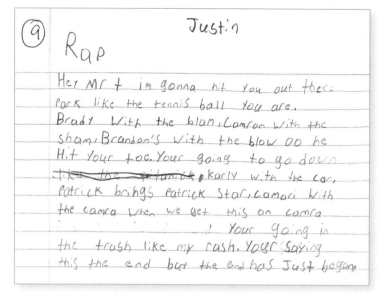

(9) Justin

Rap

Her Mr + im gonna hit you out the
park like the tennis ball you are.
Brady With the blam, Camron with the
sham, Branson's With the blow oo he
Hit your toe. Your going to go down
~~like the titanick~~ karly with the car,
Patrick brings Patrick Star, Camari With
the camra when we get this on camra
_____ d Your going in
the trash like my rash. Your saying
this the end but the end has Just began

Figure 17.2 Justin's Rap

121). As the conference unfolds, this starts to feel like a genre-specific teaching point, so I attempt to broaden it to teach him to think about word choice and finding the right word, even if the word doesn't fit a pattern.

When I suggest that Justin could talk to Amari about her word choice, Justin agrees but goes one step further. He shows me a place in his memoir where he was intentional in his chosen word. The sentence reads, "I knew she wouldn't just magically appear. I wanted her to." When he points out the word *magically*, we can see how he is transferring this craft idea of intentional word choice across genres—which is exactly what we hope for in a craft unit.

Rationale for the Study

In this unit students will explore and try out crafting techniques that will make their writing more engaging for a reader. In many ways this unit is similar to Reading Like a Writer (Chapter 5). In both units, students notice techniques authors use and try them out. But Reading Like a Writer is primarily a process unit, focused on the habit of mind (process) of trying out whichever craft techniques students notice, rather than on specific techniques we hope they'll try.

Video 17.1
Justin's Conference

In a craft study, we do care about which techniques students notice and try out. Teachers will focus on all sorts of techniques and strategies writers use to make their writing interesting and engaging to readers. Of course, these techniques show up in many genres since—as Katie Wood Ray would say—craft cuts across genre. By allowing students to choose their genre and showing the same crafting technique in multiple genres, we can help students understand how the techniques they've learned in one unit can be used in another.

There are some categories of crafting techniques that could be units of their own, including punctuation and structure, which are presented as stand-alone units in this book (see Chapters 18 and 19). Others, such as beautiful language and word choice, could also be stand-alone units.

→ **You might choose this study if . . .**

- *You don't have a punctuation, structure, or language unit in the year.*

- *You want to support your students in crafting more engaging text.*

- *You want to support your students' ability to read like a writer (to notice and try out crafting techniques).*

Grade Range

K–6. The types of crafting techniques studied become more sophisticated as we go up through the grades and students become more intentional and articulate about the crafting techniques they are using, but a craft study works in any grade.

Time of Year

This unit could be placed at any point in the year. In kindergarten, I would leave it until later in the year, when students are able to try out more in their writing. In other grades, if the unit comes early in the year, students can use the techniques they focus on in subsequent writing throughout the year.

Student Learning and the Writing Celebration

Since the goal for this unit is for students to try out specific techniques they have noticed, we will want students to display their learning during the celebration. Students could show the piece of writing (published, teacher, or student) that inspired them to use a particular technique as well as where they tried it out. While students might share their whole piece of writing, they could just share a technique(s) they intentionally used.

Key Unit Question

What genre are you writing in, and what crafting techniques have you used to make your writing more engaging?

This question helps reinforce that this unit focuses on trying out various techniques regardless of genre.

Gathering Published Mentor Texts

The stack of published texts for this unit will vary depending on which crafting techniques you want students to notice. If you are focusing on a variety of engagement techniques, you might look for texts that include multiple techniques, such as beautiful language, interesting text features (manipulated font or interesting layout, for example), various uses of punctuation, and obvious structures.

You might also decide to narrow the range of techniques students notice by focusing your selection. For example, you might decide not to focus on punctuation as a crafting tool since punctuation is a separate unit of study in the following grade, and you might leave out structure because it's studied in depth the year before. It's not that you couldn't include those. It's just a decision you will have to make.

You might decide to include some pieces of published writing that you have already used with your class in other units. When students are familiar with a piece of writing, it's easier to focus on noticing techniques rather than on the content. Basically, it's easier to read like a writer when you have already read like a reader. You might also use pieces of writing you plan to use later in the year so students will recognize them when you use them in a later unit. And, depending on which genres you study throughout the year, you might want to add some pieces of writing from genres you don't study to open up the possibilities of additional genres.

What Might I Teach?

Primary Goal

Students will show evidence of noticing and trying out specific techniques to make their writing engaging.

Possible Teaching Points

Immersion

During the immersion days students start noticing techniques in your chosen stack of texts. You might start with the whole class noticing techniques in one text together. Depending on how well they already read like writers, more or less modeling of noticing techniques will be helpful. Then you might have students work with a text in partnerships to notice crafting techniques. Partnerships can share what they noticed with the class while you add what they've noticed to your anchor chart.

You might choose to spend another day noticing techniques as a whole class, adding to the list and starting to categorize the techniques into groups. You might also show some samples of your own writing and student writing that use some of the techniques from the list. Showing them samples of teacher and student writing helps reinforce the idea that this unit is focused on using the techniques, rather than just noticing.

The techniques you choose for minilesson topics will obviously depend on the age of your students.

Beautiful Language

- Careful word choice
- Strong verbs
- Interesting adjectives
- Paired adjectives
- Specific nouns
- Revision for word choice
- Interesting sentence structure
- Sentence variety—length and complexity
- One-word sentences
- Figurative language—similes, metaphors, alliteration, onomatopoeia
- Repetition
- Multiple actions in a sentence (often three)

Layout, Manipulated Font, and Text Features

- Varied text and illustration placement from page to page
- Manipulated font size
- Manipulated font layout
- Words that are s-t-r-e-t-c-h-e-d out so readers will read them more slowly

- **Bold** print
- Words in ALL CAPS
- Speech bubbles
- Use of white space on the page to get your reader to pause

Punctuation

- Multiple punctuation marks!?!
- Punctuation that gets your reader to pause—ellipses, commas, dashes, semicolons
- Various uses of exclamation points

See Chapter 18 for more punctuation topics.

Obvious Structures

- Seesaw (back-and-forth) structure
- Movement through time—days of the week, months of the year, hours of the day, seasons
- Repeated lines structure
- Question-and-answer structure
- Endings that go back to the beginning
- Endings that break a pattern

See Chapter 19 for more structure ideas.

Process

- Taking risks—trying techniques out
- Using moderation—not overusing a particular technique (avoiding the understandable and predictable "if one ellipsis is good, fifteen are better" syndrome)
- Revising for a technique and living with it for a while to see if you want to keep it or change back to what you had originally (a good strategy for reluctant revisers)

As always, these lists are meant to open up possibilities for individual minilessons, rather than limit them. You and your students will find many additional techniques.

Conferring

What to Carry with You

While you will need to have published texts, your own writing, and student writing samples, in this unit you might rely on published writing a bit more. The techniques you'll study are easily noticed in published text. The type of writing students will encounter most often during the year is published text, so using published mentors in conferences supports their ability to notice what published authors do and try it out in their own writing.

Students will also need to see what it looks like when students in their class try techniques out, so you will want to start saving and using student samples.

What to Think About While Conferring

In any unit of study (including genre studies), there is an advantage to looking at the writing of the students you will confer with that day before writing workshop starts (over lunch, before the school day starts, etc.). It will be particularly helpful to look at student writing in advance in this unit since it is easy to see what techniques students have been trying. It also gives you a head start on narrowing down what you might teach. When looking at the writing in advance, you might ask yourself:

- Which techniques has this child tried already?

- Which techniques might work well in this piece of writing?

- Which techniques would stretch this child as a writer?

Maya's conference focuses on a specific technique, but it grows into a bigger idea (Video 17.2). I'm thrilled to learn that Maya is writing a series of books with her friends Evie, Ella, and Adrian. It's empowering to have this type of writing honored in school. Maya also has an authentic purpose for her writing: selling their books by the side of the road (with a bit of adult supervision). I love this image of Maya and her friends setting up shop and people stopping to buy their books. After listening to her writing, I decide to show her how she could manipulate her words to affect how they sound to a reader. I use a published how-to article about kicking a soccer ball to

Video 17.2
Maya's Conference

It fowlows Me ①

The death of MY friend

MY life was : changed when
I was a kid, To be exdt when
MY brother passed away. 10 years
later I was at a party with
all MY friends. After the party
I had weird vibes, I got home
and went to bed. when I was
dreaming I saw a black figure.
Also with a freind named Alice.
sorry got to pause MY name
is natile. back to the story
Alice dieing. I got out of bed
and dashed to Alices house, But
sadly when I got there I saw
a path of blood, I called The Police
an abulance also came. Her sister
elice said "were am I going to
go now". "You will go to foster
care". I went howme to ball
MY eyes out. I talked on
the Phone with the rest
of MY friends, then the
line cut of I tried to
turn the wifi back on
but it would not work.

It fowlows Me ②

(A deathly letter)

I tried to get the wifi back on. But
it would not turn on. so I forgot it.
The next day I went to school when
I got back there was a letter I opened
it it read: dear natile rerlember Your promis
Your freind eatlan. "But I never made a
Promise" natile sead very Panicked. she talked
it over with her parents. They said I shoud
go to aant luna's basicly casile. I only
stad I would if MY freinds could go
with me. They of corse the loving parents
that they are said yes. the next
morning I paked. when I was near
dresser I went over to MY bed and
found another letter. I opened it read:
Dear natily remember You Promised this
is.. the last straw. they drove the car
to Aunt luna's. when me and MY freinds
got there the stupid seuratery came
and said "impontment" ritht behind her
came aunt luna. I said hi and my
friends and I got sutuated. After
that I went to the librdy to find
a book. And found a letter that
reasi dear natile I have been waiting

Figure 17.3 Maya's Story, Pages 1 and 2

show her how the author used bold print, all caps, and an exclamation mark to change how the word "**GOAL!**" sounds to the reader.

I then go beyond this specific technique into the more powerful idea of making sure what's on the page matches your voice. When Maya reads the sentence "'But I never *made* a promise,' Natalie said, very panicked," she emphasizes the word *made*, but there's nothing on the page to indicate that (Figure 17.3). So we talk about not just how she could change that but also how authors make sure the print matches the intended voice. It's important not to lock ourselves into a particular teaching point before starting. Once you talk with and listen carefully to the child, you may decide to support the child in using a technique that you hadn't considered, or you may decide to teach them something about planning, revision, or editing.

For More on This Unit

- *The Big Book of Details: 46 Moves for Teaching Writers to Elaborate* by Rozlyn Linder

- *Craft Lessons: Teaching Writing K–8*, 2nd ed., by Ralph Fletcher and JoAnn Portalupi

- *Strategic Writing Conferences: Smart Conversations That Move Young Writers Forward* by Carl Anderson

- *Wondrous Words: Writers and Writing in the Elementary Classroom* by Katie Wood Ray

Chapter 18

Using Punctuation as a Crafting Tool

or

Using Interesting Punctuation

or

Techniques Writers Use to Affect How Their Writing Sounds

When you watch Video 18.1: Minilesson on Punctuation, a clip of the very first lesson in a second-grade class' study of techniques writers use to affect how their writing sounds, you hear one child exclaim, as the class notices all the places author Nicola Davies gets her readers to pause in the book *Bat Loves the Night*, "I think she's doing that for a reason!" Which is, of course, the unit's big idea—authors use punctuation intentionally to show how they want us to read the text.

This aim of the lesson in the video is to make sure students have time to write on the first day. Rather than functioning as an introduction to immersion, this lesson simply sets the stage for students to notice and think about punctuation before they go off to write. The following day, this class did spend writing workshop time working in partnerships to notice punctuation in books, rather than writing. This initial lesson sets the stage for their inquiry work in the following lesson. You might decide to do both on the first day, however.

This introductory lesson runs a bit longer than a typical ten-minute minilesson, which makes sense since students are engaged in inquiry and the lesson is setting the stage for the unit. In those fifteen minutes students quickly build on what they already know about punctuation and start thinking about the decisions published authors, and eventually student authors, make.

Video 18.1
Minilesson on Punctuation

As you watch the lesson unfold, you'll notice several other things happening that relate to unit goals:

- Students notice how Nicola uses white space and skips lines to get her reader to pause—which brings up the issue of whether, in a unit like this one, you will focus strictly on traditional punctuation or also include other techniques that work in similar ways (bold print, etc.).

- When a child sees an ellipsis and calls it a "dot dot dot," I honor their language—but also layer in the term *ellipsis*. In this unit, understanding what punctuation *does* is of primary importance, but I tend to introduce the punctuation's correct name as well.

- During this first lesson, you'll see that I hold off on clarifying for another child that a hyphen and a dash have different names, but we do explore what that dash does and whether it does what a hyphen does.

Rationale for the Study

In this unit students will notice how authors use punctuation to affect the meaning of their writing. They will try out punctuation moves (and perhaps other techniques) in their writing. Conscious use of punctuation is among the many techniques writers use to strengthen voice, engage readers, and make writing interesting. Word choice, structure, language, and punctuation are used in concert to make writing interesting to read.

Whenever I talk with author and writing expert Katherine Bomer, she reminds me that conventions are not separate from meaning. Punctuation *directly influences* meaning, so rather than studying punctuation in isolation, it's more informative and authentic to examine how punctuation affects a text in context.

This unit is particularly inquiry driven—students themselves notice and examine how authors use a wide range of different punctuation moves to affect meaning. While a by-product will be that students use punctuation more correctly, that's not the main focus. It's important to remember that correct use of conventions—like punctuation—can be a goal in every genre, craft, and process unit of study throughout the year (Glover and Berry 2012).

You will decide whether you want to study techniques beyond punctuation that affect how writing sounds, especially in the primary grades. For example, manipulating font size so your audience reads text louder or softer isn't technically using punctuation, but it has a similar impact. Your students might notice related techniques in other units, or you might include them in this unit.

→ **You might choose this study if . . .**

- *Your students aren't making intentional decisions about using punctuation, or they think that correctness is all that matters in punctuation,*

- *Your students aren't using a variety of different types of punctuation.*

- *You want to increase your students' ability to notice how authors use punctuation (and possibly other techniques) to affect how their writing sounds.*

Grade Range

K–6. I've included kindergarten in the grade range, though punctuation isn't a unit I'd rush to have in kindergarten, since there is not so much work to be done with punctuation when there is less text on the page.

Time of Year

This study could occur any time of year. Particularly in the primary grades, students will have more to try out when they have more text on a page, so the study will be more meaningful if you wait until your students are ready. In the upper grades, it might go early enough in the year so that students could continue to use their deeper understanding about punctuation in subsequent units. Because punctuation tends to be a shorter unit of three to four weeks, it can also be used to break up a string of genre studies.

Student Learning and the Writing Celebration

Throughout this unit students will show evidence of conscious use of punctuation moves and techniques, and also explain which authors they learned these techniques from. At the celebration, students will share their writing, but in addition they could

- show the most interesting and powerful punctuation move in their writing;

- highlight a portion of their writing that particularly shows what they learned about punctuation;

- show a place where they tried out different types of punctuation to get their writing to sound just right.

A Word About Conventions Study

Many teachers plan for conventions studies, or "making your writing easier for people to read" studies. Most teachers, regardless of grade level, have similar concerns about students' correct use of conventions, including spacing, capitalization, spelling, grammar, and punctuation. I understand the impetus for making this its own unit of study. If you do plan for a conventions study, allowing students to choose their genre within that unit can bring energy into a unit that by nature may not be the most engaging. While I understand the desire for a conventions unit, especially in kindergarten when we are helping children learn how to get text on the page, another way to address conventions is to increase the amount of time you spend *in each unit* on conventions and to teach into each child's particular conventions needs in conferences.

During the celebration, we want to be careful not to take away from the main goal of sharing and celebrating students' writing. Connecting their writing to the unit goals is important but should be subsidiary to students' sharing.

You could, of course, choose something else for students to highlight, but during the celebration you should have some easy way for students to show evidence of what they've learned. Depending on the grade, you could let students know early on in the unit that they will be showing their punctuation moves during the celebration; the older the students, the earlier you could let them know. We want students writing with the end goals in mind.

Key Unit Questions

What have you done in your writing that affects how your writing sounds?
    or
What is the most interesting punctuation decision you have made in your writing?

Gathering Mentor Texts

This stack of mentor texts is relatively easy to find. You might start by looking through stacks you've collected for other units. In the primary grades your stack will consist of picture books, while in the intermediate grades you'll collect pieces of writing from short stories, articles, essays, and anything else you study across the year. You'll also want to include examples of genres you don't plan to study, to broaden the range of what students might choose to write.

When thinking about the content of the books in my stack, I'd include a picture book that gets across the importance of what punctuation *does*. Chris Raschka's *Yo! Yes?* does this quite well. I might also look for books that have interesting or unusual punctuation like the "!?!" that you find in *Don't Let the Pigeon Stay Up Late!* by Mo Willems.

This unit is a good example of why it's helpful to know what units you plan to include in your year. As you examine texts for other units, you can keep an eye out for interesting uses of punctuation. By the time you get to your punctuation unit, you will have pieces of writing that students already know, which makes them easier to use.

What Might I Teach?

You can decide whether to focus solely on how traditional punctuation affects the meaning of writing or to broaden the inquiry to include techniques that aren't technically punctuation but also affect the sound of writing—for example, **bold print**, the use of white space to get your reader to pause, and manipulated font.

Primary Goals

Students will use punctuation to more effectively craft text and create meaning.
    or
Students will intentionally use a variety of different types of punctuation to enhance text, both in this unit and throughout the year.

Possible Teaching Points

Immersion

While an immersion phase isn't crucial to this unit, since presumably students have been using punctuation all along, I do recommend a day or two of immersion for a punctuation study. This allows students to inquire into texts to notice how authors use different types of punctuation. When students start writing on day three after two days of being immersed in this kind of inquiry, they start using different types of punctuation right away—much more quickly than if they had received a ten-minute minilesson about punctuation on day one of the unit and then started writing.

In the primary grades, you might read *Yo! Yes?* or another book with varied, easy-to-notice punctuation to get the unit started, and then send partnerships off with a book to see what types of punctuation they notice. You might want to tell them that they don't need to notice periods and can use sticky notes to mark any other types of punctuation they find. Older students can do the same kind of noticing with all types of writing, but in addition to just *finding* punctuation, they might also talk about what they think the punctuation *does*. At any age, students don't need to know what a punctuation mark is called. The fact that punctuation is so visible and easy to notice in texts makes this an excellent activity for students to do with a partner.

The earlier minilessons in the unit might focus on punctuation moves that are easier to try out.

General Punctuation

- Trying out punctuation in your writing

- Using punctuation intentionally (We want students to move from just trying a punctuation mark out to being able to explain why they made that choice.)

- Not overusing certain punctuation moves (Many students, especially younger students, quickly think that if one ellipsis is good, fifteen are better.)

- Reading your writing aloud to see if what's on the page matches your voice

- Listening to your partner read your writing aloud to see if it sounds the way you want
- Revising for punctuation
- Answering the question "What's your most interesting punctuation move?"

Getting Your Reader to Pause

There are multiple punctuation marks that get a reader to pause, for different reasons.

- Ellipsis for suspense, anticipation
- Ellipsis to get your reader to pause, as in *Sail Away* by Donald Crews
- Ellipsis at the end of a sentence, as in *Hug Me* by Simona Ciraolo
- Ellipsis followed by a period, as in *Bat Loves the Night*
- Colons
- Dashes
- Commas (What we teach about commas would depend greatly on the age of the students.)
- White space on the page (if you go beyond punctuation)

Punctuation for Emphasis

- Exclamation point so a reader will read the words louder
- Exclamation point for emphasis (*Night at the Fair* by Donald Crews has a great exclamation point to show emphasis, or a sense of wow.)
- Exclamation point to show a sense of relief (The only word on the last page of *Sail Away* by Donald Crews is "Moored!" which indicates a sense of relief that the boat has made it safely through the storm and is anchored safely in the harbor.)
- Combinations of punctuation (such as "!?!" in *Don't Let the Pigeon Stay Up Late!* by Mo Willems)
- Bold print (if you go beyond punctuation)
- Words in all caps (if you go beyond punctuation)
- Words s-t-r-e-t-c-h-e-d out to be said slowly, or crunched together (if you go beyond punctuation)

Correct Punctuation

Since the focus of this unit is on crafting with punctuation, you might spend very little, if any, time on periods, question marks, apostrophes, or use of commas in a series. However, depending on your goals for other units in the year and how your students already use punctuation, you could have some minilessons on how to use punctuation correctly. This could even be the focus of a unit, but that's a different unit of study.

Punctuating Dialogue

Deciding whether or not to teach into punctuating dialogue is an interesting decision teachers will have to make since this is a craft study and students will be writing in a variety of genres—some of which may not include dialogue. You may decide not to teach into punctuating dialogue in this unit and save it for a narrative writing unit. Dialogue and quotation marks can show up in essays and informational articles with quotes, but students may not be using many quotes in this unit. While there is a lot to teach about crafting dialogue (not overusing *said*; placing the name of the speaker at the beginning, middle, or end of a sentence; breaking up dialogue with action; implying rather than explicitly stating who is speaking, etc.), there's also not a lot of room for growth in how to use quotation marks to indicate what is being said. You might teach older students how to include punctuation with the dialogue and how to use commas related to dialogue, but again, you might save that for a unit based on some type of narrative writing.

Contractions and Apostrophes

It is likely that younger students will notice contractions, and you could certainly study them. While choosing to use a contraction or not affects writing's tone, it is not a punctuation craft move that has a lot of bang for its buck. You might choose to simply *notice* contractions and apostrophes and name what they do, but not teach into them at this point.

Conferring

What to Carry with You

During conferences, I recommend carrying with you several pieces of writing from your stack of mentor texts, from several different genres. It is particularly easy to see what punctuation does in a published text, and often teachers have a go-to piece of writing for a particular punctuation move.

You will also need samples of your own writing to show where you have tried out interesting punctuation or where you are planning to try it out. You could use pieces of your own writing from other units in the year that represent a variety of genres. You might also start a new piece in a genre the class hasn't studied or in a genre that you think students might want to try out.

While it may be easier for students to clearly see punctuation in a published text, it is always powerful when they see a peer using it in their writing. Just because they can see it in a published text doesn't mean they can have a vision for how to use it in their own writing. Some students will be more apt to try something when they see it in another student's writing.

What to Think About While Conferring

The first thing to look and listen for in conferences is evidence that students are using punctuation to craft text. You might start each conference by asking students about their punctuation decisions. Once you understand their thinking, you can help them use punctuation more effectively. You might teach into any of the lesson topics I've suggested or something else suggested by your conversation with that student.

Second-grader Ava is in the class from the minilesson in the opening of this chapter. Since she's in a punctuation study, I start the conference thinking I might end up teaching into punctuation, but of course there are other possibilities. In the beginning of Ava's conference (Video 18.2), I notice

- what Ava understands about genre when she says, "I'm making a book that's not ever going to happen";

- how she's thinking ahead in her writing and that I might teach into planning;

- how she found her topic;

- what goals she has for herself as a writer (end punctuation) that I could teach into;

- how she's already using interesting punctuation (three exclamation points).

If I knew Ava better, I might have done less research into her thinking, but I wanted to be as informed as possible as I considered a range of teaching points. I decide to teach Ava how to make sure her punctuation matches how she wants her writing to sound, which is a goal for this unit. I teach this by showing her how I do this in my own writing (teacher writing as a mentor) with my book about my daughter Molly. I also have with me a book about my dog Duncan and could have used that, but I didn't want Ava, who is writing about her dog, to think that the teaching point is related to the topic—and I didn't want to give her the impression that mentor texts need to be about the same topic as your writing is. When Ava tries this out with the title of her book she reads it differently than she did originally, but her voice still doesn't quite match three exclamation marks, so I help her envision the difference by reading her writing out loud two different ways. By saying, "Does that sound like one exclamation point or three?" I'm helping her see the impact her punctuation choices have on her readers.

At the share time later that morning, we look at Ava's title (Figure 18.1) and show how it sounds with three exclamation points (Video 18.3: Share Time: Punctuation). Knowing how many exclamation points you need isn't a goal for the unit, of course, but using punctuation to help make your writing sound the way you want it to is. The students join in, showing how three exclamation points make the title sound, which helps reinforce the unit focus right from the start.

For More on This Unit

- *About the Authors: Writing Workshop with Our Youngest Writers* by Katie Wood Ray and Lisa B. Cleaveland

- *Mechanically Inclined: Building Grammar, Usage, and Style into Writer's Workshop* by Jeff Anderson

- *More About the Authors: Authors and Illustrators Mentor Our Youngest Writers* by Lisa B. Cleaveland

- *Practical Punctuation: Lessons on Rule Making and Rule Breaking in Elementary Writing* by Dan Feigelson

- *Study Driven: A Framework for Planning Units of Study in the Writing Workshop* by Katie Wood Ray

Video 18.2

Ava's Conference

Video 18.3

Share Time: Punctuation

My dog!!!

Lucia wanted A dog. She said MOMI Want a dog. her mom Said okay" get our brother. She said ok Lucia got her brother ⅓ they went to the ⅓ Pet Shop.

pet shop

When Lucia went insid there was so many kinds of dogs!! But when she looked at one she said that one her mom Said okay ⅓ then they boght things. or it'

Figure 18.1　Pages from Ava's Book

Chapter 19

Using Text Structures as Crafting Tools

or

Using Structure to Make Writing Engaging

Hannah, a kindergartner, is making a book about bugs. She has structured her writing using a back-and-forth / compare-and-contrast form. Her first page says, "Butterflies are pretty." Page 2 says, "Bumblebees are not." She keeps this structure going ("Caterpillars are nice. Mosquitoes are not," etc.) throughout her book. Her class had noticed many different obvious structures, and she chose this one.

Jeremy, a fifth grader, used the same structure as Hannah in his essay about why *Fortnite* is better than *Minecraft*. Rather than just give all the reasons why Fortnite is better, Jeremy started with a reason why *Fortnite* was good (there's an element of danger) and why *Minecraft* was bad (if you're going to build something, you should use real objects). His essay alternates between the good and the bad, firmly coming down on the side of *Fortnite*.

In his commentary "Your Team . . . . My Team . . . . ," Rick Reilly (2003) uses the same structure as Hannah and Jeremy do. He compares views on referees, stadiums, and so on from the viewpoint of "your team" and "my team."

> *THE PARENTS ON YOUR KID'S SOCCER TEAM are ref-baiting loudmouths who need to get a life.*
>
> *THE PARENTS ON MY KID'S SOCCER TEAM are fully engaged in the lives of their children.*

At any age, in different genres, authors sometimes use obvious structures to engage their reader and to convey a message more strongly.

Rationale for the Study

In this unit students will learn how to use predictable structures to craft texts that engage a reader and convey a clear message. Just as with other techniques, interesting structures can engage a reader. Structure can be studied at any time, but we accelerate students' understanding of using structure as a crafting tool by exposing students to a variety of text structures in the context of a discrete unit.

All texts have some kind of structure. Informational writing is often structured into sections, and narrative writing is often structured by sequence or time. In this unit, though, the focus is on obvious, predictable text structures—as the organizing principle of both an entire text and a smaller part of a long, complex piece of writing. Often, the power of these structures comes from repetition or the predictable nature of the text. In the book *Loki and Alex*, Charles R. Smith Jr. alternates between what the boy Alex sees and what the dog Loki sees. It takes only two pages to figure out how the text works and start anticipating what's coming next. Writing that has a clear structure appeals to the part of our brains that seeks patterns and order. There are many different types of structures we might study, including, but not limited to

- obvious movement through time—days of the week, months of the year, seasons, hours of the day;

- back-and-forth or compare-and-contrast structure;

- question-and-answer structure;

- number or ABC structure (whether it's a counting book or an ABCs of skateboarding article);

- building structure (as in *The Napping House* by Audrey Wood);

- repeated line structure;

- list structure (think top ten lists).

In the younger grades, you'll find books with obvious structures throughout your classroom and school library, especially books by favorite authors like Eric Carle. In upper grades, you can look in magazines, in newspapers, and online.

As students grow as writers, they will use these structures in more sophisticated ways. Older students might select a structure to make a point, while younger students might use one to make their writing more interesting to read.

While this unit could appear in any grade, I want to make a quick point about it in kindergarten. I sometimes see this unit early in the kindergarten year as a predictable text unit (rather than a text structure unit) in which students write "I like _____" books or "I see _____" books. While these kinds of books do have predictable text, the structure is not used to engage the reader. Teachers often choose to include this type of unit because students are reading these types of predictable texts. I would actually *not* include this unit, for several reasons. New readers have access to these types of books (hopefully not as their entire reading diet) because the pattern supports them as they work to figure out the text. This is a helpful reading support—but these structures don't support them in composing engaging writing. Young writers need access to more sophisticated texts than those they can read on their own, to expand what is possible in their writing. For some time, young writers can write at a higher level than they can read at, so we would need to use more complex writing samples. The predictable language also reduces student thinking and decision-making. We want to expose students to a variety of structures and have them choose one they want to try. Requiring all students to write in the same structure is counter to the goal of having students consider and choose a structure. But there's an even bigger reason I wouldn't include a predictable text unit in kindergarten. It would send the message that children are limited to what they can write conventionally. We wouldn't have three- and four-year-old children compose predictable language for their illustrations, and it is similarly limiting to ask five- and six-year-olds to compose this way.

→ **You might choose this study if . . .**

- *You want to help your students understand that they can write about the same topic using different structures.*

- *You want your students to focus on a particular strategy to engage a reader.*

- *Your students need support in organizing their writing and thinking ahead.*

- *You want your students to understand that the parts of a text work together.*

- *You want to deepen your students' understanding of the idea of structure in any genre, even when the structure is less obvious.*

Grade Range

K–6. This unit could appear in any grade. If I included it in kindergarten, I would save it until later in the year. Of course, the sophistication of the writing will increase as children get older.

Time of Year

This unit could be placed at any point in the year. You could wait until later, when students have more text on the page and have more to structure, especially in kindergarten. But, if you placed this unit earlier in the year, students would benefit from their deeper understanding of structure in subsequent units of study.

Student Learning and the Writing Celebration

The focus for this celebration might be on the connection between the structure and the mentor texts. Students at any age could display the mentor text that inspired their structure along with their own writing.

Students might also reflect on how their structure helped make their writing more engaging. They might share their reflection at the celebration or write it in their notebook and have that notebook page open during the celebration.

Key Unit Questions

What structure have you chosen, and why?

or

How is the structure you've chosen working?

Gathering Mentor Texts

Many picture books follow a predictable structure. From *The Very Hungry Caterpillar* by Eric Carle (days of the week) to *City Dog, Country Frog* by Mo Willems (seasons of the year) to *Grandpa Never Lies* by Ralph Fletcher (repeated line and seasons) to *What Do You Do with a Tail Like This?* by Steve Jenkins and Robin Page (question-and-answer structure), these kinds of books are probably already on your shelf.

The big question for primary-grade teachers is which structures to represent in your stack. I usually shoot for four to six structures rather than ten to fifteen. I want to make sure that the range of structures provides options for students at various levels of risk-taking comfort, as well as enough structures to match a variety of topics and genres. I might also not include certain structures unless I really want students to try them. For example, ABC texts can be engaging for young children but can also be laborious if students have to include all twenty-six letters (and what about *X*?). You will have to consider the issues related to any structure alongside what you know about your students.

In the intermediate grades, you can find authors who use these structures in all different types of writing. The informational articles in *Ranger Rick*, *Highlights*, and other children's magazines often use the same types of predictable structures we find in picture books. And there are short stories that have obvious time stamp structures and structures that show two points of view.

It helps if your grade-level team knows that your grade is teaching this unit well in advance so that the team members have time to look for stacks. You can find these structures by regularly (and quickly) looking through children's magazines in your school and public libraries. Plus, an online search for "a day in the life of [insert athlete or celebrity here]" will produce several possibilities. You can also find these structures in all sorts of magazines and newspapers you read at home. Once you know to look for them, you'll find them in all types of writing you read on a regular basis.

Deciding what structures to put in your stack at any grade isn't meant to strictly limit structures children might choose. A student might find a different structure on their own and decide to try it out. The point of including just a few in your stack is that there's an advantage to studying slightly fewer structures in depth rather than studying every possible structure superficially.

You might also want to collect several examples of the same structure being used in different kinds of texts, especially for older students. You might make connections between a structure in a book they know from early grades and the same structure in a more sophisticated type of writing. For example, you might remind students of the hours of the week structure they loved in Eric Carle's *The Grouchy Ladybug* and point out that they can see the same structure in an article that takes readers through a day in the life of Steph Curry.

What Might I Teach?

Primary Goals

Students will try out various structures to engage their reader.

or

Students will consider which structure aligns with their genre and topic and use the structure to produce a piece (or a section of a piece).

Possible Teaching Points

Immersion

At any grade, you'd want to immerse students in the experience of noticing structures in text, since predictable structures are easy to see. During these days, you'll study texts together. This is a great unit for partnerships to do a lot of noticing and reporting out to the class. To deepen older students' noticing, you might help students consider how many parts the structure has or whether the structure changes.

You might also focus some of the conversation on thinking about why the author chose this structure and what makes this structure engaging. What is the impact of the structure on the reader?

It's also helpful, during this stage, to show students what it looks like when you try out a structure and what it looked like when other students tried out a variety of structures last year. Ideally, show examples of the same structure in different genres.

Early in the Unit

- Choosing a structure to match your topic and purpose

- Planning your writing in advance based on your structure

- Trying out several structures for the same topic in your notebook (intermediate grades)

- Starting your writing when you are using a structure (Will the writing start with the pattern, or will there be a bit of an introduction before the pattern starts?)

- Elaborating within a part of the structure

- Using the same structure to write about a new topic

- Writing about the same topic using a different structure

Exploring Various Structures

- Movement through time—hours of the day, days of the week, months, seasons

- Repeated lines or phrases

- Back-and-forth or compare-and-contrast structure

- Question-and-answer structure

- Endings that take you back to the beginning

- Movement through a place

- ABCs, numbers, or colors as a structure

Across Structures

- How to maintain your structure throughout the writing

- How to write beginnings when using a structure (How much, if any, writing occurs before the predictable structure starts?)

- How to write endings when using a structure (Will the ending break the pattern? Often it does.)

For title suggestions, see *About the Authors* by Katie Wood Ray and Lisa B. Cleaveland (2004), page 182, and *Study Driven* by Katie Wood Ray (2006), pages 262–64.

Conferring

What to Carry with You

You will need to carry a couple of published mentor texts with you, but your own writing will be important in this unit. You may want to have several pieces of your own writing on the same topic but with different structures. You might also want to start a piece of your own writing with a structure from your stack but in a different genre.

What to Think About While Conferring

In the primary grades, you'll be looking for evidence that students are trying out structure in very elementary ways. It will be important to not get too caught up in teaching into the structure and to disregard the quality of the texts. Young students tend to focus only on the structure, sometimes to the detriment of composition and meaning. So, while the first thing you'll look for in conferences is how students are using a structure, you can also help students improve their writing even if they are using the structure in a very approximate way. When conferring, you can support elaboration, word choice, sentence variety, revision, and other skills within the structure the child has chosen.

In my conference with Maren, a typically bouncy kindergartner, I see that she has chosen a simple structure for her book about cakes (Video 19.1). She tells the reader the name of the cake (Figure 19.1) and then elaborates by adding a sentence describing it, something her teacher showed her to do. I notice that when we get to the money cake (only in kindergarten!), the book stops. In many (not all) books with a predictable structure, the ending breaks the pattern and lets the reader know the book has ended.

I use two mentors to help Maren see this. I show her how in *Cookie's Week* by Cindy Ward (which goes through the days of the week), Cookie the cat doesn't cause a mess on Sunday like he does on every other day. I then show her my book about my twin daughters that goes back and forth between what they like to do and what they don't like to do. I break the pattern on the last page by writing, "Molly and Natalie are good friends."

I've shown Maren two mentors, but I'm not sensing that I can just walk away. It's not that I'm going to require her to add an ending that breaks the pattern, but I'm not sure I've given her support to try this out if she chooses. So I ask her what she is going to write (oral rehearsal), and she says she's not sure. I decide do some envisioning of possible ways she might end her book, but before I can get through the first one, she suggests she might end with "I love cake." I go ahead and envision a couple of other possible endings. I decide to stay and watch her start writing her new ending. My sense is that I probably don't need to continue this conference

Figure 19.1 Maren's Book

Video 19.1

Maren's Conference

any longer, but I am curious as to what she'll write. Maren's conference isn't typical because I used two mentors: published and teacher writing. Usually in a conference I show just one mentor, but on occasion I will show two. In this case I wanted her to see endings in two different structures.

This unit lends itself to focusing on thinking ahead and planning. Very young writers need to think about a structure before they start. We should be comfortable when young children produce very approximate structures (they may lose the structure along the way, for example), but we can certainly help them think ahead. It's certainly easier to use a days of the week structure if you decide that up front and think ahead before you start writing.

As children get older, we expect their planning to be more complex and sophisticated. Upper-grade students will need to plan not only for the genre they have chosen but also for their structure within it. For example, I showed a fourth-grade class how I was planning for a story about my dog Milo that was going to have the repeated line "Milo was new to being in a family." I had to think about where the repeated line could occur so that it would be spread out evenly across the story. Before I started, I also had to think about how the line might change the last time it was used. Combining genre planning and structure planning will help children be more thoughtful and take more ownership over the planning process, since their plan may look different from their classmates' plans.

⟶ **For More on This Unit**

- *About the Authors: Writing Workshop with Our Youngest Writers* by Katie Wood Ray and Lisa B. Cleaveland, pages 172–82

- *Poems Are Teachers: How Studying Poetry Strengthens Writing in All Genres* by Amy Ludwig VanDerwater

- *Study Driven: A Framework for Planning Units of Study in the Writing Workshop* by Katie Wood Ray, pages 262–64

Chapter 20

Author Study

or

Studying an Author's Craft

or

Author Study: Noticing, Naming, and Trying Out

Ariah's class has been studying a favorite author of first graders, Mo Willems. They've spent time noticing the crafting techniques Mo uses in his books, as well as thinking about his writing process. The students have also been using these techniques in their own books, in both the illustrations and the words.

I believe that Ariah is the type of writer who notices and tries out what other authors do, so at the beginning of Ariah's conference (Video 20.1) I ask, "What have you tried in your writing that you learned from Mo?" Ariah has an answer ready: she uses many different colors in her writing. As we look closer at her funny story, I point out other Mo techniques she has used, even if she wasn't aware of it. I show her how she uses speech bubbles, a common Mo technique. I also notice how she is showing movement in her illustration, just like Mo does. She is rather pleased by all these similarities!

I decide to build on her ability to use techniques she has noticed by showing her how Mo uses different techniques for the same purpose. In addition to using motion lines like Ariah, Mo also draws the *Knuffle Bunny* character Trixie with multiple arms and lines to show flapping. Ariah recognizes this technique and says, "Mo unfroze his characters." I also show her how Mo sometimes shows characters frozen in midmotion. I end by asking Ariah where she might try this illustration technique in her writing. The goal for this unit is to support students in noticing techniques and trying them out, and Ariah is certainly meeting this goal. Learning from mentor authors will serve Ariah well as a writer, at any age and in any type of writing.

Video 20.1

Ariah's Conference

Rationale for the Study

In this unit students will become better writers by noticing techniques an author uses and trying them out in their writing. In many ways, an author study is related to a reading like a writer study (Chapter 5) or a general craft study (Chapter 17) because all three of these units have a strong focus on noticing what published authors do and trying those techniques out in one's own writing. The difference with an author study is that we are now studying a specific author(s). Usually students study one author, although I know some teachers who focus on one author for part of the unit and then another author for the rest of the unit. I also know some teachers who study two authors concurrently throughout the unit and examine similarities and differences between the two.

Another variation on this unit could be for students to decide on an author they want to study. When teachers structure the unit this way, they usually narrow it down with the class to three to five authors to study. Students then form groups based on the author they want to study. If you choose to organize the unit this way, read the tips in the sections below.

Throughout this book I have talked about published mentor texts. But Ralph Fletcher (2011), Lisa B. Cleaveland (2016), and others make the case that we are actually learning from mentor *authors* and the decisions they make as they write—not just the texts. Studying carefully the craft of a mentor author helps us understand both the process and the techniques authors use.

A key decision, then, will be which author to study. The first thing to decide is whether you want to make this a unit that allows for choice of genre. Of course, whenever I have a unit that *potentially* provides the opportunity for students to choose their genre, I want to take advantage of it. Here are a couple of options for mentor author studies that ensure children can choose their genre:

1. Choose an author who writes in more than one genre. I always have to be careful about this because I sometimes fall into the trap of thinking that a particular author writes only in one genre, or I'm not aware of the full range of genres they write in. For example, I associate Kevin Henkes with books like *Wemberly Worried* and *Chrysanthemum*, and if I put only books like these in my stack, it would be a genre study. But instead, if I also included *Birds* or *In the Middle of Fall* by Kevin Henkes in my stack, it would be a craft study that allowed for choice of genre.

   Some authors are easier to do this for than others. If you choose an author who writes in many different genres, like Cynthia Rylant, Marla Frazee, or Nicola Davies, you can easily build a cross-genre stack. For other authors, it may take a bit more searching to find other genres. But as long as your stack has more than one genre represented, the texts students are studying won't imply that students can write only in one genre.

2. Choose an author who writes in just one genre, but show students how the crafting techniques they notice can be used in other genres. To do this, you would need to have several pieces of your own writing from genres different from the genre represented in your stack of text. For example, you might include a poem you

wrote. The language and description used by poets transfer into most genres. Throughout the unit you would also show student examples from a variety of genres. If you were to do this, you might need a minilesson early in the unit about choosing your genre.

While either option will work, there are some advantages to studying a single author. Studying a single author's craft can strengthen children's connection to an author and their image of themselves as authors. There is also an advantage to studying something in greater depth, which requires students to look beyond more surface-level crafting techniques.

If your students individually or in groups choose an author, your teaching will be heavily focused on reading like a writer, rather than on a particular author's craft.

→ **You might choose this study if . . .**

- *You want to improve your students' ability to notice more deeply as they read like a writer.*

- *There is an author your students particularly love.*

- *You want students to study both an author's process and how an author crafts texts.*

Grade Range

K–6. Authors studies seem to occur more frequently in the primary grades, but learning from a mentor author can benefit students in any grade. Even as an adult, I study favorite authors' craft.

A closely related unit is the process study Independent Genre Study (Chapter 9). In that study, in addition to gathering a stack of a genre, students could gather a stack of one author's writing, then notice and try out that author's techniques.

Time of Year

This unit could be placed at any point in the year.

Student Learning and the Writing Celebration

As in many of the craft studies, in addition to sharing writing at the celebration, students could also show a technique they learned from the author they were studying—they could display the technique both in their own writing and in the published text.

They might also show how their process was similar to or different from that of the author they studied. For example, if students heard an author talk about how they planned their writing, students could show their own planning and how it was similar to or different from the author's.

Finally, it's important to celebrate approximations. We're not expecting students to use a technique as well as a published author. Therefore, students might highlight a technique they tried for the first time, or a technique that was particularly challenging, to allow us to value their risk taking as much as or more than their skill in using the technique.

Key Unit Question

What have you tried in your writing that you have learned from _____ [author you are studying]?

Gathering Mentor Texts

The texts (from your author) you choose for this unit will determine whether this is a craft study (choice of genre) or a genre study. In addition, there are some other considerations when choosing an author to study:

- Make sure that you choose an author you want to spend the next four weeks with. Your students will quickly ascertain whether this is an author you love or not, and your energy for studying the author will influence students' engagement.

- Choose an author who uses crafting techniques that are appropriate for the age of your students and will help them become better writers. This sounds obvious, but I occasionally encounter teachers who are studying an author because they like the author, rather than because the author's craft will be instructive for students. For example, I know kindergarten teachers who study Jan Brett. I love Jan's stories, but I would really have to examine them to think about which techniques Jan uses that kindergartners could use. Children love the borders of her illustrations, but would drawing intricate borders help children become better authors? I'm not saying I would or wouldn't study Jan Brett. I'd just have to really consider which techniques students would benefit from noticing and trying out.

- Choose an author who uses techniques that you can easily envision students noticing and trying out. In *More About the Authors*, Lisa B. Cleaveland (2016) suggests you choose an author with an easily identifiable style. I know many primary-grade teachers who choose Mo Willems because he uses so many techniques that are easy for children to notice and try out.

- If possible, study an author who uses a range of techniques of varying complexities. For example, in *Grandpa Never Lies* and *Marshfield Dreams*, Ralph Fletcher uses some techniques that are easy to see and some that are more subtle, which allows for various depths of noticing.

If your students are forming groups that will each study one of three to five authors, you will need to think about your stack differently. You will need to help students collect a small stack of texts from their author. This should be fairly easy since they are choosing authors they already know and love. Also, if students choose an author to study, you will need to think about which texts you will use for your minilessons. I would not think that you would teach separate lessons to each author-based group. We're teaching about noticing and trying out, not the specific author. Instead, your minilessons would focus on *how to study* the group's author. Organizing the unit this way tilts it to being more similar to the intermediate-grade process study Independent Genre Study (Chapter 9). For your minilessons, you could use these strategies:

- Choose a completely different author from the authors students chose, and use that author for modeling how to notice and try out.

- Alternate between the authors students chose. For example, in your minilesson on noticing word choice, you could use Kevin Henkes (one group's author), and in your minilesson on noticing manipulated font, you could use Mo Willems (another group's author).

You'll also want to study the author's process, not just their writing. When you're choosing an author, you might look for video clips, social media posts, or interviews. If you're not sure if an author will work, try it out and see how it goes. If you decide an author doesn't work as well as you'd hoped, students can always study that author as readers rather than as writers.

What Might I Teach?

Primary Goals

Students will notice and intentionally try out techniques from a specific author.
    or
Students will notice and try out techniques from a specific author and use them throughout the year.

The assessment of this second goal stretches beyond the unit. We don't want students to try out techniques for this unit and then stop. In subsequent units you might have a goal about using techniques noticed in the author study.

You can have teaching points beyond those related to unit goals (planning, revision, conventions, etc.).

Possible Teaching Points

Immersion

In this unit students will benefit from both whole-group noticing and noticing with partners. The first day might start by reading a text together, first as a reader and then as a writer. But then students could work in partnerships with a text to notice techniques to share with the class and add to the class' anchor chart.

Noticing and Trying Out Crafting Techniques

Much of this unit will consist of students noticing techniques and trying them out in their writing. Noticing and trying out won't necessarily happen on the same day since we don't want students forcing techniques into their writing. Ideally students will try out techniques when appropriate, and we certainly expect them to use multiple techniques.

The actual techniques you focus on will vary greatly depending on the grade you teach and the author you choose. Rather than a list of techniques, here are some categories to look for. You can also get more specific lesson topics in Chapter 17.

- Word choice

- Layout and text features

- Sentence variety

- Techniques that affect how writing sounds

- Punctuation

- Obvious structures

- Beautiful language, figurative language, and sensory language

- Beginnings and endings

Author's Process

While there are some broad commonalities in how authors work, individual authors' processes can be very different. If you were to watch all the video clips in one of the sections of the companion website, www.authortoauthor.org, you would see how authors' processes vary in terms of finding ideas, choosing genres, planning, talking with others, and revision.

General Guidelines for Using Techniques

- Using the anchor chart to try techniques out (if students are noticing but not trying out)
- Using techniques intentionally
- Not overusing techniques
- Noticing techniques an author uses in multiple texts or in a single text

Conferring

What to Carry with You

Since this unit focuses on specific authors, I use published mentor texts more frequently. It's also important to collect your own writing and student samples that show how various techniques are used.

For students who are having trouble trying things in their own writing, a particularly effective move is to use a child in the class who has tried the specific technique already. When we pull one child over to show another child how they tried something out, both students benefit. In fact, increasingly I am using less confident writers to be the mentor for a more confident writer, which lifts the less confident child's status as a writer in the class.

What to Think About While Conferring

The first thing you will want to notice in a conference is which crafting techniques the child is using. If the child isn't using any, then you might show them a technique they could use or teach them how to try techniques out. If the child is already trying techniques out, you could help them try out more sophisticated techniques or techniques that are harder to notice.

Let's think back to Ariah's conference (Video 20.1). You can see me first asking her which techniques she tried. Since she clearly is trying out techniques, I go deeper by helping her expand her range of techniques.

I also help Ariah understand what she is doing by specifically naming a technique. When I ask Ariah how Mo Willems shows motion, she says, "He made it look like he was running." Being this general is very common. It's kind of like saying, "You need more detail in your writing"—it's not specific enough. I help her understand the more specific technique by naming exactly what Mo did—he drew the leg in a bent position. One of our jobs as teachers is to help students move from the general to the more specific, which makes a technique easier to try out.

I also do some envisioning for Ariah. I ask her where she might try this technique out, and she's not sure. I envision for her that she could show the person running after the luggage or the tears moving down the character's face. Many teachers are overly cautious about not wanting to tell a child what to write. I certainly want Ariah to make decisions, but she just said she doesn't know how to transfer this new idea into her book. I help her see possibilities, without taking ownership of her writing.

In Ariah's class, students haven't yet noticed this new way of showing motion. Or course, you don't have to wait for a process or crafting technique to be taught in a minilesson in order to show a child how to try it out. And then Ariah is ready as a mentor, so that students can be like Ariah, just as they're trying to be like Mo.

If you are organizing the unit by having students choose an author to study, remember that when you are conferring you don't need to teach with that author's stack, because you are focusing on how and what to notice, not on the specific author. You're not trying to teach four different author studies at the same time.

⟶ For More on This Unit

- *About the Authors: Writing Workshop with Our Youngest Writers* by Katie Wood Ray and Lisa B. Cleaveland

- *Mentor Authors, Mentor Texts: Short Texts, Craft Notes, and Practical Classroom Uses* by Ralph Fletcher

- *More About the Authors: Authors and Illustrators Mentor Our Youngest Writers* by Lisa B. Cleaveland

- *Writing with Mentors: How to Reach Every Writer in the Room with Current, Engaging Mentor Texts* by Allison Marchetti and Rebekah O'Dell

Published Mentor Text References

Amazing Powers by Catherine Saunders

American Girl series

Baseball Saved Us by Ken Mochizuki

Bat Loves the Night by Nicola Davies

Birds by Kevin Henkes

Chris Paul by Jeff Savage

City Dog, Country Frog by Mo Willems

Cookie's Week by Cindy Ward

The Day the Crayons Quit by Drew Daywalt

Dog and Bear: Two Friends, Three Stories by Laura Vaccaro Seeger

Dogs by Emily Gravett

Don't Let the Pigeon Stay Up Late! by Mo Willems

Dylan's Day Out by Peter Catalanotto

Elephant and Piggie series by Mo Willems

Fly Guy series by Tedd Arnold

Frog and Toad series by Arnold Lobel

Froggy series by Jonathan London

Frogs by Gail Gibbons

Grandpa Never Lies by Ralph Fletcher

The Grouchy Ladybug by Eric Carle

Harry Potter series by J. K. Rowling

Harry Potter: A History of Magic by J. K. Rowling

How to Heal a Broken Wing by Bob Graham

Hug Me by Simona Ciraolo

In the Middle of Fall by Kevin Henkes

Jabari Jumps by Gaia Cornwall

Knuffle Bunny: A Cautionary Tale by Mo Willems

Loki and Alex by Charles R. Smith Jr.

Long Shot by Chris Paul

Marshfield Dreams by Ralph Fletcher

Mud by Mary Lyn Ray

The Mysterious Tadpole by Steven Kellogg

The Napping House by Audrey Wood

Night at the Fair by Donald Crews

No, David! by David Shannon

The Old Lady Who Swallowed Fly Guy by Tedd Arnold

Pigeon series by Mo Willems

Pokémon series

Polar Bear, Polar Bear, What Do You Hear? by Bill Martin Jr.

Red Sled by Lita Judge

Roller Coaster by Marla Frazee

Sail Away by Donald Crews

Sea Turtles by Gail Gibbons

Snow by Cynthia Rylant

The Snowy Day by Ezra Jack Keats

Tough Boris by Mem Fox

Twilight by Stephenie Meyer

The Very Hungry Caterpillar by Eric Carle

Walk On! by Marla Frazee

Wemberly Worried and *Chrysanthemum* by Kevin Henkes

What Do You Do with a Tail Like This? by Steve Jenkins and Robin Page

Who Would Win? series by Jerry Pallotta

Wonder by R. J. Palacio

Yo! Yes? by Chris Raschka

Zombie in Love by Kelly DiPucchio

Works Cited

Anderson, Carl. 2000. *How's It Going? A Practical Guide to Conferring with Student Writers.* Portsmouth, NH: Heinemann.

———. 2008. *Strategic Writing Conferences: Smart Conversations That Move Young Writers Forward.* Portsmouth, NH: Heinemann.

———. 2018. *A Teacher's Guide to Writing Conferences.* Portsmouth, NH: Heinemann.

Anderson, Jeff. 2005. *Mechanically Inclined: Building Grammar, Usage, and Style into Writer's Workshop.* Portland, ME: Stenhouse.

Anderson, Jeff, and Deborah Dean. 2014. *Revision Decisions: Talking Through Sentences and Beyond.* Portland, ME: Stenhouse.

Angelillo, Janet. 2005. *Making Revision Matter: Strategies for Guiding Students to Focus, Organize, and Strengthen Their Writing Independently.* New York: Scholastic.

Buckner, Aimee. 2005. *Notebook Know-How: Strategies for the Writer's Notebook.* Portland, ME: Stenhouse.

Cleaveland, Lisa B. 2016. *More About the Authors: Authors and Illustrators Mentor Our Youngest Writers.* Portsmouth, NH: Heinemann.

Cruz, M. Colleen. 2004. *Independent Writing: One Teacher—Thirty-Two Needs, Topics, and Plans.* Portsmouth, NH: Heinemann.

Feigelson, Dan. 2008. *Practical Punctuation: Lessons on Rule Making and Rule Breaking in Elementary Writing.* Portsmouth, NH: Heinemann.

Fletcher, Ralph. 1996. *Breathing In, Breathing Out: Keeping a Writer's Notebook.* Portsmouth, NH: Heinemann.

———. 2003. *A Writer's Notebook: Unlocking the Writer Within You.* New York: HarperCollins.

———. 2011. *Mentor Authors, Mentor Texts: Short Texts, Craft Notes, and Practical Classroom Uses.* Portsmouth, NH: Heinemann.

———. 2013. *What a Writer Needs.* 2nd ed. Portsmouth, NH: Heinemann.

———. 2017. *Joy Write: Cultivating High-Impact, Low-Stakes Writing.* Portsmouth, NH: Heinemann.

Fletcher, Ralph, and JoAnn Portalupi. 2001. *Writing Workshop: The Essential Guide.* Portsmouth, NH: Heinemann.

———. 2007. *Craft Lessons: Teaching Writing K–8.* 2nd ed. Portland, ME: Stenhouse.

Glover, Matt. 2009. *Engaging Young Writers, Preschool–Grade 1*. Portsmouth, NH: Heinemann.

Glover, Matt, and Mary Alice Berry. 2012. *Projecting Possibilities for Writers: The How, What, and Why of Designing Units of Study, K–5*. Portsmouth, NH: Heinemann.

Horn, Martha, and Mary Ellen Giacobbe. 2007. *Talking, Drawing, Writing: Lessons for Our Youngest Writers*. Portland, ME: Stenhouse.

Heard, Georgia. 2014. *The Revision Toolbox: Teaching Techniques That Work*. 2nd ed. Portsmouth, NH: Heinemann.

———. 2016. *Heart Maps: Helping Students Create and Craft Authentic Writing*. Portsmouth, NH: Heinemann.

Hertz, Christine, and Kristine Mraz. 2018. *Kids First from Day 1: A Teacher's Guide to Today's Classroom*. Portsmouth, NH: Heinemann.

Hindley, Joanne. 1996. *In the Company of Children*. York, ME: Stenhouse.

Johnston, Peter H. 2004. *Choice Words: How Our Language Affects Children's Learning*. Portland, ME: Stenhouse.

Lane, Barry. 2016. *After the End: Teaching and Learning Creative Revision*. 2nd ed. Portsmouth, NH: Heinemann.

Linder, Rozlyn. 2016. *The Big Book of Details: 46 Moves for Teaching Writers to Elaborate*. Portsmouth, NH: Heinemann.

Marchetti, Allison, and Rebekah O'Dell. 2015. *Writing with Mentors: How to Reach Every Writer in the Room Using Current, Engaging Mentor Texts*. Portsmouth, NH: Heinemann.

Mermelstein, Leah. 2013. *Self-Directed Writers: The Third Essential Element in the Writing Workshop*. Portsmouth, NH: Heinemann.

Miranda, Lin-Manuel, and Jeremy McCarter. 2016. *Hamilton: The Revolution*. New York: Grand Central.

Parsons, Stephanie. 2007. *Second Grade Writers: Units of Study to Help Children Focus on Audience and Purpose*. Portsmouth, NH: Heinemann.

Ray, Katie Wood. 1999. *Wondrous Words: Writers and Writing in the Elementary Classroom*. Urbana, IL: NCTE.

———. 2006. *Study Driven: A Framework for Planning Units of Study in the Writing Workshop*. Portsmouth, NH: Heinemann.

———. 2010. *In Pictures and In Words: Teaching the Qualities of Good Writing Through Illustration Study*. Portsmouth, NH: Heinemann.

Ray, Katie Wood, and Lisa B. Cleaveland. 2004. *About the Authors: Writing Workshop with Our Youngest Writers.* Portsmouth, NH: Heinemann.

———. 2018. *A Teacher's Guide to Getting Started with Beginning Writers, Grades K–2.* Portsmouth, NH: Heinemann.

Reilly, Rick. 2003. "Your Team . . . . My Team . . . ." *Sports Illustrated,* September 29. www.si.com/vault/2003/09/29/350530/your-team-my-team.

Robb, Laura. 2010. *Teaching Middle School Writers: What Every English Teacher Needs to Know.* Portsmouth, NH: Heinemann.

VanDerwater, Amy Ludwig. 2017. *Poems Are Teachers: How Studying Poetry Strengthens Writing in All Genres.* Portsmouth, NH: Heinemann.

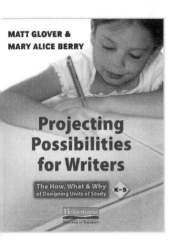

Grades K–5
978-0-325-04192-6
$20.50

Projecting Possibilities for Writers

The How, What, and Why of Designing Units of Study, K–5

Co-authored with Mary Alice Berry

As a teacher, you value instructional flexibility because, after all, nearly anything can happen—and does! Yet you still have to plan instruction that helps your writers meet curricular objectives. Helping you solve this dilemma is what *Projecting Possibilities for Writers* is all about. Matt and Mary Alice show how to project rather than plan—to design instruction to support deep understanding, to respond to individual needs, and to meet key writing standards.

I *Am* Reading
Nurturing Young Children's Meaning Making and Joyful Engagement with Any Book
Co-authored with Kathy Collins
Grades PreK–1 • 978-0-325-05092-8 • $23.50

Already Ready
Nurturing Writers in Preschool and Kindergarten
Co-authored with Katie Wood Ray
Grades PreK–K • 978-0-325-01073-1 • $27.50

Engaging Young Writers
Grades PreK–1 • 978-0-325-01745-7 • $20.50

The Teacher You Want to Be
Essays about Children, Learning, and Teaching
Co-edited with Ellin Oliver Keene
Grades K–12 • 978-0-325-07436-8 • $27.50

Watch Katie and Matt . . . Sit Down and Teach Up Ebook
Two Master Teachers Review Their Thinking as They Confer with Beginning Writers
Co-authored with Katie Wood Ray
Grades PreK–1 • 978-0-325-04451-4 • $10.49